ADVANCE PRAISE

"We spend so much time on instructional coaching for teachers but neglect to coach our school and district leaders. This is where the real change can happen in a school district that commits to coaching its leaders. Melinda and Lorna know firsthand the positive impact of coaching school leaders, as both of them have successfully done this in their careers. When leaders become more reflective and knowledgeable about how to improve their schools, student outcomes are positively impacted. It is a must-read for any superintendent committed to improving their school system."
—JEFFREY FLEIG, PHD, SUPERINTENDENT, FOND DU LAC SCHOOL DISTRICT, FOND DU LAC, WISCONSIN

"Great school leaders don't rise alone—they have trusted coaches who challenge, support, and inspire them to reach new heights. Lorna Klokkenga and Melinda Baiza are exactly those kinds of coaches. With a wealth of experience and an unwavering commitment to leadership development, they have transformed the way school leaders grow and thrive."
—CHAD J. LANESE, EDD, SUPERINTENDENT, BUCKEYE ELEMENTARY SCHOOL DISTRICT, BUCKEYE, ARIZONA

"In *Coach Better, Lead Better: Coaching Excellence for School and District Leaders*, Melinda Baiza and Lorna Klokkenga have crafted an essential guide for educational leaders seeking to elevate their impact. With over a decade of experience in transforming school leadership through expert coaching, they offer a treasure trove of practical strategies, real-world examples, and heartfelt wisdom. This book is more than just a resource; it's a catalyst for change, proving that effective coaching is the key to unlocking leadership potential. Whether you're a seasoned leader or just beginning your journey, this book is a must-read for anyone committed to fostering growth and excellence in education. Melinda and Lorna's passion and expertise shine through on every page, making this an invaluable addition to any leader's library."

—DEVON HORTON, EDD, SUPERINTENDENT, DEKALB COUNTY SCHOOL DISTRICT, STONE MOUNTAIN, GEORGIA, METRO ATLANTA AREA

"In *Coach Better, Lead Better: Coaching Excellence for School and District Leaders*, readers will discover the profound impact effective coaching can have on educational leaders. The book brilliantly highlights the critical role of a coach in shaping resilient and innovative school leaders. It provides a roadmap for leaders and coaches to navigate educational leadership challenges with practical strategies and compelling real-world examples that can be directly applied in their context. The SIMPLE framework presented is accessible and transformative, making this resource an essential tool for anyone committed to fostering growth in themselves or others. This book is a must-read for those aspiring to elevate their leadership journey."

—SYLVIA R. REYNA, PHD, ASSISTANT PROFESSOR OF PRACTICE, UT AUSTIN, AND PRESIDENT, INCARNATE WORD HIGH SCHOOL, SAN ANTONIO

"For over a decade, Melinda Baiza and Lorna Klokkenga have been at the forefront of transforming school leadership through their expert coaching. In Coach Better, Lead Better, they distill their wealth of experience into a must-read guide for anyone committed to growth. Packed with actionable insights and real-world examples, this book reveals how coaching can unlock the full potential of school and district leaders. If you're ready to elevate your leadership and empower others, don't miss the wisdom of two of the best in the field."

—NATHALIE HENDERSON, PHD, CEO, KIPP ST. LOUIS PUBLIC SCHOOLS

"Behind every impactful school leader I've known—or had the privilege to be—is a coach who shows up with both courage and compassion. In my own journey through school leadership, I've experienced firsthand how the right coaching relationship can unlock potential, shift mindsets, and sustain you through the challenges no one warns you about. Being a school or district leader is hard work, but when you have a coach behind you offering practical strategies, relatable stories from the field, and guidance on how to approach the work, it suddenly becomes doable. Whether you're leading a school or walking alongside someone who is, this book is a powerful reminder that coaching is essential. If you're ready to grow, reflect, and lead with purpose, this is the guide you'll want by your side."

—AMANDA DEBELL, DEPUTY SECRETARY FOR TEACHING, LEARNING, AND INNOVATION, NEW MEXICO PUBLIC EDUCATION DEPARTMENT

COACH BETTER, LEAD BETTER

Coach Better, Lead Better

COACHING EXCELLENCE
for School and District Leaders

Melinda Baiza & Lorna Klokkenga

COPYRIGHT © 2025 MELINDA BAIZA AND LORNA KLOKKENGA
All rights reserved.

COACH BETTER, LEAD BETTER
Coaching Excellence for School and District Leaders

FIRST EDITION

ISBN   978-1-5445-4858-6 *Hardcover*
          978-1-5445-4857-9 *Paperback*
          978-1-5445-4856-2 *Ebook*

Contents

FOREWORD 13
INTRODUCTION 19

PART 1: COACHING MATTERS
1. EVERYONE NEEDS A COACH 37
2. COACHING LEADS TO CHANGE 61

PART 2: COACHING STARTS WITHIN
3. WHAT IS YOUR WHY? 79
4. BELIEFS, VALUES, AND BEHAVIORS 93
5. THE COACHING MINDSET 111

PART 3: SIMPLE COACHING
6. COACHING APPROACHES 133
7. SKILL AND WILL 147
8. THE SIMPLE COACHING FRAMEWORK 163

PART 4: CREATING A COACHING SYSTEM
9. THE FLOW OF COACHING 179
10. A CULTURE OF COACHING 193

CONCLUSION 209
ACKNOWLEDGMENTS 213
ABOUT THE AUTHORS 215

Foreword

Enduring transformation is possible when we invest in leaders striving for excellence. Everyone needs a coach, and this book will serve as your coach on advancing leadership systemically.

Leadership in education is underinvested in, yet it's essential to dramatically improve learning and expand opportunity for students. This book is critical at a time when hope feels fragile, with NAEP scores at twenty-five-year lows and economic mobility on the decline. Leadership has infectious power to spread the hope we desperately need, though to unlock this power, leaders need access to the disciplined, transformational coaching this book offers.

I met Melinda Baiza fifteen years ago, and she has heavily influenced my organization. I lead the University of Virginia Partnership for Leaders in Education (PLE), where we've helped catalyze and support some of the most impactful K–12 system transformations across the country. As recognized by RAND, our work across thirty-three states is the only K–12 leadership development effort in the country with journal-level evidence of impact. Melinda has profoundly influenced our organization's efforts to hone our coaching and thought partnership practices vital to activating systemic change. She's worked with some of the fastest-achievement-growing districts across the United States.

We've also collaborated with powerful partners like Lorna Klokkenga, who has coached school leaders across the United States to strengthen their self-efficacy and drive significant gains in student outcomes. Since becoming a certified leadership coach, she has supported hundreds of school leaders through personalized coaching that fosters sustainable growth. Her deep expertise and strategic insight continue to make a lasting impact.

Melinda and Lorna helped us support schools like one in North Dakota that moved from the bottom 5 percent to the top 50 percent. Thank you for picking up this book and investing in the leadership critical to advancing student-centered systems change.

System-level change happens when the Melindas and Lornas within your school or district—every community has them—are inspired to believe dramatic improvement is possible and are then stretched, supported, and held accountable to pursue it and build coalitions. Effective coaching creates the culture of support and accountability necessary for successful transformation.

Our success has come from continually evolving our own approach to thought partnership and coaching (which Melinda and Lorna support). We've learned that real progress happens when leaders are supported in stepping back, gaining a clearer view of their reality, understanding the root of their challenges, and identifying leadership moves to address them.

The PLE is known for helping leaders build ninety-day action plans to drive focus and execution. But over time, we've learned that success depends more on developing reflective habits, a coaching culture, and a shared commitment to learning and adapting. I recall a powerful moment with a principal and thought partner where honest reflection moved the leader to tears. The principal was accidentally not creating a safe environment for questioning progress and strategy. They realized a desire to shift from using the plan as a compliance tool to showing up to leadership team meetings anchored in understanding progress with authenticity and vulnerability. They invited collaboration to define and monitor key drivers of success and agreed to let go of other tasks. Supporting leaders in this way, at scale, leads to breakthroughs and meaningful gains in learning and opportunity across schools.

Imagine if coaching like this, grounded in purpose, reflection, and honest partnership were the norm across our schools. I'm especially excited about the SIMPLE Coaching Framework presented here and its potential to create the shifts our education systems urgently need. Melinda and Lorna have combined Maxwell's 4 Phases of Leadership with the Skill/Will Context to help coaches better understand and lift a leader's current mindset and capacity. When scaled, coaching like this can unlock the collective power of entire communities.

Melinda and Lorna have the insight, compassion, and track record to write this book. Soon after meeting Melinda, I saw her support a leader we had found resistant and guarded. Her patience, relational focus, and accountability helped him open up and build trust with his team. I've seen her use humor, humility, and candor to help leaders grow across diverse contexts: rural and urban, elementary and secondary. I've watched Lorna guide teams through complexity with piercing inquiry and deep care. She's helped leadership teams strategically optimize schedules and teacher allocations, even amid budget cuts, always keeping student learning at the center. Her ability to balance compassion with clarity enables leaders to purposefully make tough decisions. Their partnership, and the national reach of their coaching, is inspiring.

The fact that you're reading this tells me you're like Melinda and Lorna, dissatisfied with the status quo and committed to using leadership as a lever for systems change. As you read, I hope you're inspired to consider:

- How you can deepen self-awareness, empathy, and efficacy to help your team thrive
- How transformational coaching unlocks not just personal but collective change
- How the SIMPLE Coaching Framework can help you turn abstract ideas into practical action that drives student outcomes
- How to utilize Maxwell's 4 Phases of Leadership combined with the Skill/Will Context to identify and support a coachee's current level of leadership

Thank you for investing in coaching practices and systems that inspire the broad improvements and ripple effects our students need. There is no greater joy than lifting the confidence and practice of leaders positioned to help students interrupt generational poverty and shape our collective future. *Coach Better, Lead Better* will do just that by equipping coaches with the tools, strategies, and mindset to transform leadership.

—WILLIAM ROBINSON

William Robinson is the executive director of the University of Virginia Partnership for Leaders in Education (UVA-PLE). UVA-PLE is a leading national organization in increasing the collective leadership capacity of district and school teams to together create conditions where schools thrive and create enduring improvements in student learning and experiences. Under his leadership, UVA-PLE is recognized by the Wallace Foundation and RAND as the only remaining K–12 leadership development organization in the country that qualifies as evidence-based given the impact on student results in its work across thirty-three states and almost two hundred school systems.

During his over a decade as executive director, the PLE launched nationally leading services, frameworks, and research in school system transformation and leadership drivers that lead to success. Robinson's passion for education stems from growing up in the Arkansas Delta and observing how education systems fall short of delivering practices that achieve systemic equity and racial justice. Robinson has completed consultation and board support for organizations such as the DC Public Education Fund, Stand for Children, Communities in Schools, and the Achievement Network. He is a graduate of Harvard Business School and Princeton University and an alumnus of Education Pioneers.

Introduction

Lorna's first year as a middle school principal in Texas was incredibly hard. There were three schools within a school, and Lorna had to hit the ground running. She got to the point where things ran like clockwork. The middle school was recognized for being one of the best in the district. Everybody worked together. But she had no idea what she was doing. It all came together organically. Lorna didn't have the terminology to call what she did a system, but that's what she ended up creating to survive. And after that first hard year, her school thrived.

Then she was promoted to a high school and got a reality check.

Being a high school principal is like being the mayor of a small city—a small city on an island where the buck stops with you. At one point, she had 2,400 students and 135 staff members. There were police. Food service. Budgets. She felt like she was just keeping her head above water. She got so engrossed in managerial tasks that she never really got to the point of improving instruction.

Lorna's school wasn't low performing, but it wasn't high performing either. The bear of low student performance chased her through the woods, but as the old saying goes, you only need to stay one step ahead of the person behind you, right? Lorna thought, "As long as I can beat that other school, I'm okay. As long as I run fast enough, the bear won't bite me."

Melinda's story is similar.

When Melinda went from being a successful classroom teacher in Texas to a reading specialist, she got real-time training and coaching on a monthly basis from her district that gave her confidence and skills. She stepped into her new roles and thrived. She then earned her administration degree. She became an assistant principal. "My gosh," she thought as she watched her principal lead, "I could do that." She got on the fast track to promotion, serving as an assistant principal for a short amount of time before stepping into the role of principal. And when she became principal, things went off the rails.

Melinda was completely unsure of what to do. Once-a-month meetings with her district leaders now only covered operational tasks—how to meet a budget, how to write up an underperforming teacher, how to apply for a grant—but nothing about how to think as a systems leader and how to get her faculty on board with new initiatives that could help make students' learning better.

Melinda felt she was missing something, so back at her own campus, she'd call a small group of friends from other schools when she struggled with a challenge. For the most part, they were helpful, but they only gave advice from their own contexts, and there was always a slight edge of competitiveness about this advice. Because at the end of the year, the district would rate all the campuses, and every principal fought not to be at the bottom. No one wanted to give away all their secrets, or they just didn't have time to with their own fires. So Melinda was left asking herself, "How do I get to the top?" without anyone giving her a good answer.

As we both know all too well, struggling to not be the worst is, well, the worst. Unfortunately, it is a position in which many principals and other quickly rising school and district leaders find themselves. What worked as a teacher does not work as a principal. What worked in middle school does not work in high school. What worked at the campus level does not work at the district level. And since we don't understand why something worked before, we certainly can't understand why the old methods don't work now. The result is a bad case of imposter syndrome and high rates of burnout and attrition.

Just a small selection of sources shows the current picture in our education system.

A recent survey by the National Center for Education Statistics (NCES) found that over one in ten public school principals left the profession between the 2020–2021 and 2021–2022 school years.[1]

One in five Texas public schools had a new leader this past school year. Data from the Texas Education Agency (TEA) reveals over 20 percent of Texas principals left in the

---

[1] "Roughly One in Ten Public School Principals Left Profession in 2021–22 School Year," National Center for Education Statistics, July 31, 2023, https://nces.ed.gov/whatsnew/press_releases/7_31_2023.asp.

2022–2023 academic year, marking a five percentage point increase over the past decade.[2]

These numbers are not just centralized to Texas or politically conservative states. The Superintendent Lab found that between the 2022–2023 and 2023–2024 school years, attrition rates in district leadership were greater than 20 percent in fourteen states. States like Montana, Hawaii, New Mexico, Louisiana, North Carolina, and Delaware saw attrition rates of 24 percent or higher in 2023–2024.[3]

Education Week reported in July 2023 that 11.2 percent of public school principals left education.[4] This is an increase from the most recent TASB survey in 2024 and is consistent with trends over time.[5]

Other data from the National Center for Education Statistics reported in the survey include:[6]

- More experienced principals, those with ten or more years of experience, left at higher rates than those with less than three years of experience.
- Principals over fifty-five years old left their jobs at a rate of 20 percent.

---

[2] Jeremy Landa, "Employed Principal Attrition and New Hires 2011–12 Through 2022–23," PEIMS, March 2023, https://tea.texas.gov/reports-and-data/educator-data/employed-principal-attrition-and-new-hires.pdf.

[3] Micah Ward, "What the Data Says About Superintendent Turnover in 2023–24," District Administration, January 9, 2024, https://districtadministration.com/briefing/what-the-data-says-about-superintendent-turnover-in-2023-24/.

[4] Evie Blad, "What New Data Show About Principal Turnover," Education Week, July 31, 2023, https://www.edweek.org/leadership/what-new-data-show-about-principal-turnover/2023/07.

[5] TASB, "Principal Retention," August 4, 2023, https://www.tasb.org/news-insights/principal-retention.

[6] National Center for Education Statistics, "Principal Turnover: Stayers, Movers, and Leavers," US Department of Education, Institute of Education Sciences, last updated May 2024, https://nces.ed.gov/programs/coe/indicator/slb.

- Schools with 75 percent or more students of color had the highest rate of principals moving to new schools, at 7.1 percent.
- Thirty-five percent of principals reported a decrease in enthusiasm for their job.
- Eighteen percent shared that they thought about transferring to another school.

The consequences of this turnover are profound. When a principal leaves, schools lose stability, teacher morale diminishes, teachers leave, and student achievement suffers. This ripple effect extends beyond student learning. According to a University of Houston study, the cost of replacing a principal can be upwards of $75,000. This adds to the financial burden for districts already facing limited resources.

If you are a district leader, these statistics are frightening. Time and again, we hear from the district leaders we work with, "I don't have enough principals." Or "I can't find quality candidates to fill my open district positions." Or "I can't keep my leaders."

As a school leader, whether an elementary school principal with five hundred students or a district administrator overseeing thousands, there comes a time when you just feel stuck in your role, spinning your tires with nowhere to go. You don't know what to do next. You've been in your position for years, and your school continues to be low performing. You feel you aren't making a difference.

But you still want to.

Each of the above problems has its root in one thing: school and district leaders lack knowledge in the mindsets, structures, and processes that enable their schools and districts to adopt, adapt, and sustain growth. In short, we don't know how to best lead our faculty, staff, and students because we were never taught how to lead in a higher role.

School leadership roles can feel like being on a deserted island. People may not approve of your actions, but they don't always help you be better. They don't know how to help you. And that's because education has traditionally ignored the strategies for leadership development and change management that the business world has embraced successfully.

Now, as proud educators and former school leaders, we aren't advocating to turn schools into businesses—but why can't we, as educators, adapt what works in the business world to our own purposes, to develop our own people? To help our students achieve the outcomes we want for them?

There is a crisis in our school leadership pipelines. A crisis created from a lack of professional development of our school leadership. We are unaware of what we have not yet discovered. For us, there was no one there to pull back the curtain and reveal the inner workings of the system. To help us learn how people worked and behaved within that system. We couldn't get to a place in which we felt comfortable or confident leading. We thought there had to be a better way to lead. A way that allowed us to strive to be the best. To build on our assets, not stay one step ahead of our deficits. To grow into resilient leaders capable of assessing and solving problems at the system level, and happy to stay in our schools and advance.

That way is better coaching.

COACHING IS KEY

As educational leaders, we often think we should have all the answers. We don't like admitting we don't know what we don't know. Or we think we should know it and feel embarrassed when we don't. But just because you have the credential and the skills doesn't mean you can apply those skills to a new context without coaching. A student may run fast in track, but that doesn't mean he'll be successful on the football field without a coach who constantly shows him how to run on the field. Many of us definitely feel that way and get used to having all the right answers in front of our students. But a good teacher doesn't necessarily know more than their students. Even a great teacher falls far short of the knowledge contained on the internet that every student has access to in the palm of their hand. So what is a teacher for? Why, to help students learn to ask the right questions! The same goes for school leaders.

So how do we break down that imposter syndrome?

We don't need to have all the answers; we only need to know how to ask the right questions and have someone willing to help us find the answers. This method of leadership development is a process, but the results in the end are more sustainable. It's the old adage, "If you give a man a fish, he'll eat for a day. If you teach him to fish, he'll eat for a lifetime." We have to teach our leaders to fish, get them hooked, and keep them in our schools and districts to train the next generation of leaders.

The usual process of promotion in school systems is this: a leader taps a well-liked and successful teacher or staff member on the shoulder to ascend to principal, says "You'll do fine here," and then leaves them to figure it out with minimal training in the new role. The new principal's world has just gotten exponentially bigger, with more on their plate, and now they are in the position of managing their former colleagues without any idea how to orchestrate or talk to people at this level. They fall back on quick operational practices, telling people what to do instead of educating and motivating them to do it.

In contrast, coaching is intentionally collaborative. It asks questions instead of giving answers. It asks its participants to be reflective and helps them adapt to change, to recognize and build on strengths. It helps people find intrinsic motivation, the personal, internal drive to do something because they want to, because they want to get better. It helps internalize the change—and not just one change, but many changes, in a continuous flow of growth and reflection.

- Coaching helps create well-rounded leaders who build up other leaders.
- Coaching increases retention rates for leaders.
- Coaching provides an opportunity for leaders to be reflective and proactive, preventing problems before they start.
- Coaching introduces evidence-based practices that leaders can infuse directly into their daily work.
- Coaching gives leaders an accountability partner who encourages them to take the action steps that support their goals in a timely manner.

Coaching was the key to unlocking the leaders we wanted to be: leaders not stuck in the day-to-day of operations, but leaders able to facilitate the growth and leadership development of others. The one we are developing could transfer what they'd done on the ground to a system that others could follow. A system that would remain and sustain even if they weren't around to monitor it. A blueprint for successful schools.

We never got the opportunity for a do-over as principals,

but we now know how to coach other school and district leaders to reflect and understand themselves, their people, and their systems. We now know how to create and institute sustainable professional development programs in order to build leadership pipelines of prepared, confident, adaptable school principals and district administrators. We know how these systems directly impact and improve what is supposed to be the main goal of education: student instructional outcomes. And we know how the stability and confidence these systems spread throughout a school improve school culture, leadership effectiveness, and retention.

> **THE KEY TO EFFECTIVE, SUSTAINED LEADERSHIP IS EFFECTIVE, SUSTAINED COACHING.**

We coach better to lead better. That's what this book is all about!

BE BETTER

In 2019, Lorna and Melinda met in San Marcos, Texas. San Marcos was halfway between San Antonio and Austin, their respective home bases. They followed Google Maps to a Mexican restaurant in an out-of-the-way neighborhood. It took a while to navigate the increasingly narrow roads. "Are you sure there's a restaurant here?" Lorna asked skeptically. But finally they pulled up to a dilapidated little yellow stucco house with a small faded sign on a single pole out front that said simply *Garcia's*.

"Should we try it?" Lorna asked.

"These are the best places, *lo mejor*," Melinda reassured her. They walked in, and the decor took Melinda back to her grandmother's house. The tiny mismatched tables and brightly colored walls were nothing impressive. The restaurant didn't have the internet. But the tacos were outstanding.

They'd been working together as colleagues in a large district and had recently formed a business venture as partners after working as independent, full-time consultants. They talked for long hours and found they had a larger vision for the future.

"What the heck are we doing?" Melinda wondered at one point.

"We could do more," Lorna agreed.

Melinda thought for a moment, looking around at the house-turned-restaurant that so resembled her grandmother's house in Old Town in Fort Stockton. "My grandmother and my mother want us to do more."

Melinda came from a first-generation Mexican American family. Her mother was one of three, and she and her siblings lived within a five-minute drive of each other. Education was important to her mother, and she ensured her three daughters and two sons got the learning she herself did not have access to. She thought education was the key to moving beyond the limited range of small-town opportunities available to her. She wanted more for her children.

Melinda did well in high school. She was popular. A cheerleader. Her grades were good. But when it was time to figure out what to do after high school, she met with a guidance counselor who didn't know what to do with first-generation students. She told Melinda, "You'll make a great hairdresser."

"But I want to do something different than that." Because of her mother, Melinda knew she didn't want a profession that only required a trade credential. She wanted to go to college like her older brother and sister. At the time, all the brown kids were funneled into trades, while all the white kids were funneled into college. Melinda wanted to go to college. She wanted to make an impact beyond her community, partly because of her mother's urging. But her mother didn't know how to help her. She was unaware of what she didn't know; she only understood that the end goal was meant to be positive. She didn't realize there was more to getting into school than just an idea.

Melinda did figure it out. She had an older brother and sister who were her immediate models, as they had navigated college successfully. She'd go on to earn her master's degree in administration. She fulfilled roles in school leadership positions such as school leader, state turnaround program manager, director of curriculum, instruction, and assessment (chief academic officer), and an assistant superintendent role and now as a CEO for her own consulting and coaching business. That says a lot about first-generation Mexican Americans.

Lorna grew up on a small farm in Central Illinois. She was an underachiever, getting C's across the board. Her high school counselor called her into the office her senior year and told her flat out, "You're not college material." At first, Lorna was thrilled. She didn't want to keep going to school. But that idea was a nonstarter for her parents.

There was a small junior college not too far from Lorna's high school. Her parents took her to see the admissions officer, whom they knew, the first day of fall classes and got her enrolled. They brought her to the campus bookstore to buy her books. They walked her to her first college class. Their desire for something better, like that of Melinda's mother and grandmother, drove her forward.

Lorna's mother was one of nine, born during the Depression when career opportunities were almost nonexistent, especially for women. For the four daughters in the family, the expectations were clear: in case they didn't marry, they needed a way to support themselves, which meant becoming either a nurse or a teacher. Three of them became nurses, and one became a teacher, following the limited paths available to women at the time. Lorna's mother knew education wasn't just a necessity; it was the key to a better life. Lorna's father, on the other hand, had a different experience. College or trade school had never been an option for him. As the eldest son in a farming family, he was expected to stay home and work the land to support his family. Though he never had the chance to further his own education, he never wavered in his belief that knowledge could open doors that hard labor alone could not. Together, Lorna's parents instilled in her a deep appreciation for education, not just as a path to success, but as a means of changing the course of one's life.

We do what we do because all students don't have the parents we did. We want to create systems in schools that provide the opportunity for all students to be successful, even the ones who are told they'd "make great hairdressers" and aren't "college material." We had to go somewhere. Be someone. Do something. Do something more than our parents had been able to. And the key was education.

Like many of you coming to this book, we've experienced the pain of an inadequate leadership development system in education at the K–12 level. As Aristotle actually said, "Those who understand, teach." We'd suggest the phrase:

THOSE WHO UNDERSTAND, COACH.

So how can you teach others without understanding? How can you thrive when you don't know how? You can't lead well in new roles if you were never coached how to lead well in new roles, and you certainly can't coach others how to lead well if you don't know why or how you led well. As teachers, we received years of training and continued professional development. But as principals and administrators, we receive hardly anything.

Great leadership doesn't come from having all the answers; it comes from asking the right questions, listening deeply, and creating space for others to grow. *Coach Better, Lead Better* provides a practical guide for leaders who want to elevate their impact by mastering the art of coaching.

Maybe you're a principal trying to implement a new student-centered initiative that could improve state test scores, but you're struggling to get teacher buy-in. You're unsure how to lead as "the boss" when just last year, you were a teacher yourself. Or perhaps you've been in the role for a while but feel like you're falling behind amid constant shifts in state and federal accountability systems. If you're a district leader, you may be trying to support your principals in developing a systems-level mindset that drives student success, but you're unsure how to coach them effectively. Maybe you're a curriculum director trying to grow your specialists or a principal working to strengthen your instructional coaches. Whether you're leading from the classroom, the campus, or the central office, this book is for anyone who wants to grow their coaching leadership practice to drive meaningful, sustainable change.

We wrote this book to gather all the Whys and the Hows we've learned over the years as teachers, leaders, coaches, and consultants and create a practical resource for all leaders. In the following chapters, we will delve deeper into the initial steps that school leaders must take to embark on their journey of growth and development:

- Introduce mindsets open to coaching and being coached.
- Practice reflection in work sessions to discover what kinds of values and skills you bring to your leadership and coaching.
- Share coaching tools and strategies that can be applied to your own situation.
- Explore how to set actionable goals, build a supportive environment, and create a sustainable and adaptable system of coaching for developing school and district leaders.

This isn't a book that gives you a specific how-to that works for every situation every time. As practitioners we know every school and district is different, with different student populations, teachers, and goals. But the simple, generalized activities and strategies here can be adapted anywhere. As always with professional development, adapt and use what you think will be useful for your organization. We've included reflective work sessions at the ends of chapters in Parts 1 and 2 and tools as needed in Parts 3 and 4.

As a few pieces of housekeeping, we want to assure you the identities of specific schools and leaders have been anonymized through fake names and composite characters—but the situations and details we cite are real.

We do hope this book is useful to you. This isn't a book you read once, or even twice, and put on a shelf. It's a practical guide to be thumbed through when you need a bit of advice or redirection. It's a book to use as a tool for your school improvement practices. A book in which you bookmark chapters in your e-reader or dog-ear paper pages and scribble in-margin comments (just don't let your librarian see you). It's a book that will cause you to be reflective about yourself and your mindsets toward leadership. It's a book that will sometimes be challenging. But if you "do the work," as we once told all our students, you'll reap the rewards.

Leadership is not a destination; it's a process. It's about developing skills, building trust, and instilling mindsets that empower others to lead. This isn't about adding more to your plate; it's about changing how you show up. When you coach better, you lead better. And when you lead better, you unlock the potential in everyone around you, including yourself.

Get ready to lead with greater clarity, connection, and courage.

Let's be better.

Let's coach!

PART 1

Coaching Matters

CHAPTER 1

Everyone Needs a Coach

"Everybody needs a coach. Even the most successful people in the world have coaches, an extra set of eyeballs, a perspective from outside of the frame, words of wisdom from someone who's done it before, someone to help manage a dozen ideas and get you started on one."

—ATUL GAWANDE, SURGEON AND AUTHOR

Melinda was flying to Phoenix from Austin. After she sat down in her aisle seat next to a tall gentleman, she noticed everyone on the plane was staring at them. "My gosh, is it me?" she thought. "Do I have something on me?" She frantically tried to figure out what was wrong with her while people were trying to be sneaky with their phones, taking pictures and videos.

The gentleman sitting next to Melinda had his AirPods in and was watching a documentary about Johnny Manziel, a former Texas A&M football player, on Netflix. After they reached ten thousand feet, he got up to go to the restroom, and the lady in front of Melinda took a picture as he walked back to his seat. The poor man just shook his head. "Do I know this guy?" Melinda asked herself as she got up to let him reclaim his window seat. Finally, she tapped him on the shoulder and asked him, "Are you okay?"

He curled his mouth ruefully at her. "I don't mind when people take pictures of me. I just hate it when they do it and don't ask, especially as I'm coming out of the bathroom."

"Okay, I get you." She was still baffled at the attention. Her coaching honesty and bluntness coming to the fore, she stated, "I feel like I should know you."

A small smile appeared. Too casually, he said, "It's not a big deal. I'm just an Olympic swimmer."

Scrrrrrich! The record scratched on Melinda's brain. "Holy crap, are you Michael Phelps?"

"Yes, I am." His smile was wider now.

So Melinda ended up having a fabulous conversation on her flight from Austin to Phoenix.

"I'm in the process of writing a book with my business partner, Lorna," she mentioned. "One of our references is *The Right Game*, which includes you as an example of someone who leaned into their talents and strengths, since the author claimed you were built for swimming and not a sport like running."

"You're right," he agreed. "My arm span is six feet, seven inches from the tip of one middle finger to the other. I can't run more than five hundred meters competitively. But I can swim."

"You certainly can," Melinda laughed. "So how can we help people reach their highest potential?" she mused.

"I don't know how to teach this," he said, "but something has to be innate about what they're doing. When I get in the pool, I become one with the water. I can close my eyes and know how and where I need to swim, how fast I need to go, where I need to slow down. The skills have become second nature because I have a passion for it."

Melinda crinkled her brow. "Do you ever have a time when you rest? I heard you train even on Thanksgiving and Christmas."

"Why not?" he tossed back. "It's still Thanksgiving and Christmas after I train." He smiled again. "My passion is swimming, so I want to be the best I can be at it. It only helps that I have the body type, these long arms, big feet, and webbed hands that help me follow that passion." If she'd been on that plane with us, *The Right Call: What Sports Teach Us About Work and Life* author Sally Jenkins would have applauded.

Like Phelps, Jenkins encourages people to decide what they're good at and then do that. She claims that to reach your full potential, you have to find what works for you. You can't fit into someone else's mold. If you're built to be a swimmer, swim. If you're built to be a runner, run.

Most of us had someone who inspired us to be better and reach our full potential, but what's often missing from inspiring words is the training and upskilling necessary to enact that potential.

That's where coaches come in.

PEOPLE GROW MORE WHEN THEY'RE IN THE RIGHT SEAT ON THE BUS.

Since a coach's main goal is to facilitate positive growth, all we want is for our coachees to find the right seat and then make sure the people *they* coach find their seat in turn.

Both of us found it difficult to identify the right seat on our own. Life has a lot of distractions, and we were often too close to the chapter we were in to see the full story. We needed someone who could ask the questions that led us to our best skills and our most profound discoveries about ourselves.

How do you recognize issues that stand in your way if you don't have a coach to help see and name them? As a professional, how do you get better at what you do?

As leaders, we often don't frame our careers as a process of getting better. We don't think we should need a coach to support our continued growth. We think we should already understand it and beat ourselves up when we don't. We think that's just how the system is.

And we'd be right.

THE BROKEN SYSTEM

Lorna had been an assistant principal of her middle school for five years before getting tapped on the shoulder to fill the role of principal. She moved down the hall two doors and a world away to commence one of the hardest years of her life. All of a sudden, the buck stopped with her. She didn't have any additional training for this role; her supervisors just assumed she'd be good at it like she'd been good at assistant principal. Knowledge was gained on the job through trial and error, as her supervisors absented themselves from the scene. To Lorna, it felt like the attitude was "You're there. The school runs. It's just two doors down the hall. What bit of difference is that? You've got this."

For eight years, Lorna struggled with her high school, staying those couple steps ahead of the back of the pack. Then she was promoted to senior director of school improvement.

She relocated to the central office, where she was finally introduced to coaching, oddly enough, not to be coached, but to become a coach. She was provided comprehensive training at the University of Virginia Partnership for Leaders in Education, training she had not received as a principal. She learned about systems, finally understanding why certain initiatives had worked and others had not. "My Gosh," she thought, "I want to go back and do it all over again. I want to be a principal like this."

Her experience was like so many others. Many times, we've seen district leaders, out of desperation, take capable people out of staff roles like teacher or counselor and put them into leadership positions like assistant principal or principal, crossing their fingers that the competence that made them successful before will port over whole cloth to the new role. But being a teacher or counselor is a very different beast than running a whole campus. It's no longer just instructional outcomes that must be dealt with; it's also things like budgeting, discipline, and maintenance. It's ensuring a now large and diverse ecosystem of staff and faculty gets along and runs smoothly, all while working toward school improvement that impacts student achievement.

There has been a systemic failure of coaching at all leadership levels within many of the schools and districts we work with. Professional development may exist within a role, such as teaching teachers how to be better teachers, but there is limited training that teaches teachers how to be principals or principals how to be better central office leaders. In some districts we've worked with, principals haven't had consistent onboarding and training in fifteen years. And when principals do get professional development, it's concentrated on managerial or operational tasks, like how to make a budget or order parts for maintenance. There's little to no training on how to achieve instructional goals at the campus or district level or how to manage a huge group of diverse staff and students. If they struggle through well enough to get promoted to district offices, they may be in charge of promoting others to the roles they just left. But how do you coach someone else if you've never been coached yourself? The answer is, you don't. So why do we expect our educational leader to do so?

In short, administrators at district offices may not know how to coach their principals. Principals may not know how to coach their staff and faculty. Coaching provides that extra set of eyes from the outside looking in that can put a problem into perspective. Ideally, those eyes have also worked through similar problems in that same role, so the wisdom comes from someone who's been there before.

"Everyone needs a coach," as Dr. Atul Gawande, a renowned surgeon, writer, and public health researcher, says. Gawande had a coach in the operating room who suggested he move his foot so his back didn't hurt while he stood for hours doing surgery on his patients. The message here is to find someone to be your external ears and eyes, who can stand back and record what you do and show you that big picture to help you understand when things go wrong and how to fix them—or if things go right, how to keep things going right.

To get better, "get a coach," Gawande proclaims, because no matter how hard you look, you can't see yourself swing a golf club. You can't see your whole self in action. Gawande was speaking mostly of athletes, all of whom have one or even a team of coaches, but you don't have to look far to find coaches in private industry, healthcare, and politics. So why is education, where learning is sacred, the one place where leaders are haphazardly taught how to level up?

Like in Lorna's case, the lack of coaching, and therefore the lack of confidence and competence, in new roles creates confusion. The new principal or superintendent knows they have the credentials, such as newly earned degrees in administration, but they don't have the skillsets to make effective decisions in their new position.

Without guidance or further training for this new role, people tend to do what they know how to do. It follows that if a leader doesn't know what a new strategy is, how to do it, or why it works, they won't try it. No one wants to risk trying something new and failing as a leader.

But the results of not changing are untenable.

We work with districts that have been failing for years, one of which had exactly one student graduate from high school on time out of a class of over 160. Another had an 11 percent proficiency rate in English learners (EL). When we ask them, "What have you tried to increase your reading proficiency scores?" the reaction is often like a deer in the headlights: "I don't know." Everyone is looking at the data, but not everyone knows how to interpret it or turn it into actionable steps for improvement.

Right now, we recognize that many schools are working hard to create opportunities for growth and success: Title I schools with high poverty and EL, alternative schools filled with children on individual education plans (IEPs) with high amounts of trauma, behavioral, and mental health issues, and developmental delays. We may not be able to change a student's past, take away their trauma, make them less poor, or instantaneously give them a second language, but there *are* things we as school and district leaders can do to work with and through these challenges. The systems, strategies, and tools are already out there. Schools are already using them.

It's just a question of which ones may work for schools with similar problems.

This is where coaching matters. Strong leadership isn't just about knowing what to do; it's about having the guidance, support, and accountability to do it well.

> **COACHING HELPS LEADERS NAVIGATE COMPLEXITY, MAKE INFORMED DECISIONS, AND IMPLEMENT LASTING CHANGE THAT IMPACTS STUDENTS' LIVES.**

But first, we have to recognize what we don't know.

MAXWELL'S 4 LEVELS OF LEADERSHIP

Melinda may have felt like she was drowning at times, but she had enough tenacity to learn to swim on her own. It wasn't always pretty, but her school was still successful. It didn't fall to the bottom. So, as a relatively successful principal, she took a position at a service center, which operated as an arm of the Texas Education Agency (TEA). She became a turnaround manager for turnaround schools. She was good at what she did, but she didn't know how she did it. Again, she lacked the big-picture view that would reveal the system she'd organically invented and put into place. She used data to guide the changes she wanted to make but didn't know how to explain that data, exactly what it meant, or what underlying causes led to the numbers that showed up.

Her employer offered Melinda the opportunity to participate in the leadership coaching program. "Coaching?"

Melinda thought. "What are they going to coach me to do?" She had no idea she needed a coach. It felt like a bit of a blow to someone who thought she was on the right track. Reluctantly, and with no little angst about the thought of talking to someone for an hour straight about her performance, Melinda went to her sessions and found the missing piece of her leadership.

By exercising reflection, Melinda was able to finally grow as a leader. Her coach helped bring out her best by bringing up the experiences that made her a successful principal and then connecting those experiences to her position as a turnaround program manager. Once she knew *how* and *why* she'd succeeded, she could break that knowledge down into a template for other school leaders to follow. She could articulate what data was important for other principals to look at and then how to draw a line from that data to practical, on-the-ground instruction, policy, and initiatives. The potential and the skills were there; she just hadn't realized how everything fit together. Therefore, she couldn't create a blueprint for her success plan until she knew how all the parts fit together.

Melinda had to open herself to accepting coaching and being vulnerable before she could turn the questions on herself so she could support her own growth mindset.

We don't think about how all the pieces fit together, the systems of cause and effect, and we fall into the "ready, fire, aim" form of problem-solving, where we're just guessing at what solves a problem instead of finding out from data and research what the root cause of the problem is and what proven techniques and systems have been shown to solve it.

The reluctance within leadership to change may be

explained through John C. Maxwell's 4 Phases of Leadership, which break down like this:[7]

- Phase 1—I don't know what I don't know.
- Phase 2—I know what I don't know.
- Phase 3—I grow and know and it starts to show.
- Phase 4—I simply go because of what I know.

In Phase 1, the person lacks knowledge that will make them a successful leader. They don't know what the possibilities and options are that can solve their problems.

In Phase 2, the person identifies what their problems are and what knowledge they need to gain to solve them.

Phase 3, the person seeks out training from experts in the areas they need to improve and then—this is key—puts this learning into practice. This phase can be a little awkward as theory becomes application and mistakes are made and actions and behaviors are finessed until they get the results that are looked for.

Then, in Phase 4, that learning and practice become an integrated, sustainable part of the leader's values and practice and are now a skill they can put on their résumé and take and apply anywhere.

To explain why leaders can't get those they lead to change, Maxwell proposes his Five Levels of Leadership:[8]

- Level 1: Position—We see we have a problem and come up with a solution to fix it.

---

[7] John C. Maxwell, *The 21 Irrefutable Laws of Leadership: Follow Them and People Will Follow You*, 10th anniversary ed. (Thomas Nelson, 2007).

[8] John C. Maxwell, *The 5 Levels of Leadership: Proven Steps to Maximize Your Potential* (Center Street, 2011).

- Level 2: Permission—We get the go-ahead to try that solution.
- Level 3: Production—We get things done by applying our solution and check to see if it's working.
- Level 4: People Development/Reproduction—Potential leaders are identified and shown why this solution works, are taught this solution, and try it themselves.
- Level 5: Pinnacle/Sustainability—Leaders turn into coaches and invest their lives into other leaders for the long haul, leaving a legacy of leaders behind who apply this effective solution; it becomes part of the culture and no longer needs managerial oversight to be implemented.

In Maxwell's model, we've found education leaders often get stuck at Level 3. School and district leaders are really good at going from expectations to actions. They get a below-average literacy score. Executive leaders determine how they're going to raise those scores, say, by a superintendent's goal of 40 percent. The executive leaders go back to their principals and say, "This is what I want you to do: increase your scores by 40 percent." But the big questions left unanswered in this quick action model are telling: Why are the scores low to begin with? Where is the breakdown in literacy learning? What evidence-based practices exist that address that particular breakdown? And how is that practice going to be implemented? How are teachers going to be taught and supported through that new initiative?

When there's a lack of reflection, solutions become "ready, shoot, aim." Leaders go straight to the goal instead of doing the work to find out what best accomplishes that goal. And then we wonder why our changes don't work. Level 3 is often where leaders get stuck if the solution that was thought up in Level 1 has no basis in reality because it actually doesn't fix the root cause of the problem or doesn't take aim at the problem like we thought.

Successful leaders, on the other hand, look at the root cause of the problem all the way back at Level 1. They ask questions like, What is the real problem we need to solve? What's only a symptom, and what's the real cause or causes of a bad outcome? What do we really need to do to solve this problem? For instance, a student might be distracted and unable to concentrate on their reading in class not because the teacher's pedagogy is at fault, but because the student is hungry, which was shown in studies that linked free lunch programs to improve student performance.[9] Or the data shows that students are doing better with literacy scores when they are tested by a teacher than when they are tested by a tablet, so maybe the problem isn't literacy at all, but the way students are being tested.

Part of the goal of coaching is to help leaders identify why a problem exists and what solution would best address that underlying problem—to help leaders diagnose a disease and not just react to a symptom. To effectively address challenges, leaders must go beyond surface-level fixes and engage in deeper analysis. A coach plays a crucial role in this process by guiding leaders through reflection, helping them ask the right questions, and providing an outside perspective to uncover patterns and key leverage points. With the right coaching support, leaders can move from reactive decision-making to strategic, sustainable solutions. Consider these probing questions:

---

9   Allie Pearce and Anona Neal, "Challenges and Opportunities of Providing Free School Meals for All," Center for American Progress, September 26, 2023, https://www.americanprogress.org/article/challenges-and-opportunities-of-providing-free-school-meals-for-all/.

- What is the data, both current and historical, telling us?
- What potential solutions exist in similar conditions as ours that could work for us?
- What condition is in place to create a change that will last and address the root cause of a problem?
- How do we get everyone primed and willing to make this change?
- Do we have the resources and bandwidth to make this change and set up the conditions for its success?
- And most importantly to Levels 4 and 5, how do we create a system around the change that will work over the long term?

Since schools often get stuck on Level 3, there is little to no chance of advancing to Levels 4 and 5, which is common in well-run businesses and companies in which leadership pipelines actively cultivate and coach promising employees to become company leaders in their own right. For instance, H-E-B, Texas's beloved grocery store behemoth, has a leadership academy that educates staff through various leadership levels. You can't walk into an H-E-B and become a floor manager; you have to progress through their levels, learn their culture and operations from the ground up, before you can lead and train those beneath you. Since schools often promote from within their ranks as well, a leadership academy model might work well in those spaces too.

Larger school districts have caught on to these business models and are starting to adapt them to their own leadership needs. High-level teachers who want to be leaders are identified early and developed even as they teach, or assistant principals are hired who want to be principals.

For example, one district we coached implemented an

Aspiring Leadership Academy that identified sitting assistant principals and teachers who were working toward their master's in educational administration and wanted to be promoted to higher roles. We then helped interview and select twenty of these candidates for a first cohort. They committed to a two-year leadership training process that included pedagogy training for creating effective teams and organizational leadership assessments to identify leadership competencies and how to best leverage them. We also worked with the district to identify district systems that the new leaders would need to know, such as budget software, and we familiarized the cohort with those systems so they'd be able to navigate them in the future.

Much of this wasn't sexy, but it was all things the district leaders needed to know about to be successful. To support this work, we provided coaching to several members of the first cohort, equipping them with the skills and strategies needed to navigate these challenges effectively. The key component to any of these leadership academies, business or education, is the mentorship and coaching that goes on between existing leaders and developing leaders within those programs. If you don't invest in the system of coaching that produces the outcome of good leaders, you end up with stagnant growth and missed opportunities.

As of this writing, the district's program was discontinued due to a change in funding and district leadership, a common issue with initiatives, which meant there wasn't enough time for the district to get to Maxwell's Level 5, which is when a program and pipeline get institutionalized and become sustainable without outside guidance. Which points to another detriment of high leadership turnover: change isn't given enough time to settle in before real results can be measured.

Much of professional development in schools is one-and-done workshops. Something new is introduced, but then there's no follow-up or support to make those suggested changes in the classroom or on campus. Many great ideas have been abandoned before they could gain traction.

Once people know what they don't know, they still need help to internalize that knowledge. Coaching helps with that transition. They can read about it, but that doesn't mean they can go do it after one day of training. That doesn't mean they're going to come back from that training and do it because someone told them to. Tomorrow, the teachers or staff will go back to their classrooms and buildings, and guess what will happen? They won't think about professional development from yesterday. Those precious notes from the day before will get put away and never looked at again. Workshops that prompt participants to practice the tools and skills and provide applicable takeaways that can be put into place the next day help with transferring those skills to a new context, but those small tool-sharing sessions may only go as far as an individual. They can't change pedagogy or an instructional system wholesale like coaching can. Workshops can get you to Level 4, where you simply know what you're supposed to do and you do it, but it's hard to transfer that to new contexts and grow it across the district without assistance.

THE THREE M'S: MONEY, MANPOWER, MOTIVATION

Instituting a professional development coaching plan and leadership pipeline doesn't happen overnight. There is no quick fix to systemic problems—any systemic problems. Trying something out for a few months and not following through on the work, not making it a deep-seated part of the school's culture and operations, leads to failure. While relationships are essential to the success of coaching, it takes time to build a positive relationship. Developing people takes time. But we'll say one thing:

DEVELOPING PEOPLE WITH EXPERIENCED COACHING PRODUCES MORE EFFECTIVE LEADERS FASTER THAN LEAVING THEM TO FLOUNDER ON THEIR OWN.

And when leaders lead well, everyone down the chain benefits, including teachers, staff, and students.

Leadership academy programs are still few and far between in education, mainly because of lack of money, manpower, and the motivation to get the pipeline started and through to Level 5, at which point it sustains itself.[10] There are always limited funds available, especially for Title I schools that have a higher number of competing initiatives and priorities. Lack of funding goes hand in hand with lack of manpower. The schools can't afford to hire extra helping hands or provide the higher salaries other districts do. But a sense of support, professionalism, and opportunities for training and advancement may keep people on the job even if pay isn't the highest.[11] As data supports the importance of professional development opportunities, it may be time for

---

10 Susan M. Gates et al., *Principal Pipelines: A Feasible, Affordable, and Effective Way for Districts to Improve Schools (RAND Corporation, 2019)*, https://doi.org/10.7249/RR2666.

11 "Exploring the Relationship Between Employee Training Opportunities & Turnover Rates," Awardco, July 2, 2024, https://www.awardco.com/blog/exploring-the-relationship-between-employee-training-opportunities-turnover-rates.

businesses like yours to consider ways to cultivate paths for employees to grow.[12] "The bottom line is that any organization that doesn't provide development incentives to their people is not optimizing its human capital," Warren Buffett, CEO of Berkshire Hathaway, says. "These days, you can't afford to not develop your employees."

Money is closely linked with the opportunity for leaders to train. Here in Central Texas, there are many opportunities and programs, both within schools and districts and through partner universities and programs, to learn new skills, whereas smaller private, charter, and rural schools may not have the funds or programs nearby to support their leaders' growth. Even large school districts may not choose to spend their money on developing their leaders. Teachers, as those closest to students, often get regular professional development. But for one of the districts we worked with, it was the first time in fifteen years that they invested in their leaders. Out of 130 principals, there had been 5 that received prior training a decade and a half ago. Everybody else was new, and they'd all had to make it up as they went along.

Motivation is the biggest piece schools and districts have control over. Many districts know they need succession plans, as they seem to spend an inordinate amount of time hiring for new vacancies, and tenure in these positions is only four years on average.[13] Beyond hosting workshops or making symbolic efforts, truly addressing the root causes of poor

---

12 "Business Leaders Explain How Professional Development Benefits Help with Employee Retention," University of Massachusetts Global, October 21, 2019, https://www.umassglobal.edu/blog-news/business-leaders-explain-how-professional-development-benefits-help-with-employee.

13 Stephanie Levin and Kathryn Bradley, *Understanding and Addressing Principal Turnover: A Review of the Research* (National Association of Secondary School Principals and Learning Policy Institute, 2019), https://www.nassp.org/wp-content/uploads/2020/06/nassp_edit06-WEB.pdf.

retention, such as constant overwhelm and lack of support, often takes a back seat—which leads us to our next question. What makes educational leadership coaching worth investing a district's money, manpower, and motivation?

BENEFITS OF COACHING

There is a bucketful of research across industries and higher education that points to the benefits or return on investment (ROI), to use a business term, that coaching produces for a school district.

> Among the principal characteristics most strongly associated with job stability is educational experience, including preparedness for the position as a result of preparation and/or in-service programs and having an advanced degree. Better-prepared principals, including those who have had internships and/or mentors, are less stressed and stay longer, even if they are in high-need schools.[14]

Relatedly, some evidence suggests that principals who are viewed as more effective by teachers and supervisors are less likely to leave unless they are promoted. Researchers suggest that perhaps because these principals feel more efficacious, they feel better about their work and are more likely to stay. Both findings suggest the importance of supporting principals in building their capacity to do the complex work required in their schools.[15]

---

14 Levin and Bradley, *Understanding and Addressing Principal Turnover*.

15 National Association of Secondary School Principals, "Principal Shortage," accessed May 13, 2025, https://www.nassp.org/principal-shortage.

In the business world, where coaching is more prevalent and well studied, the story is much the same. A Fortune 500 company studying the ROI of executive coaching found that 77 percent of respondents indicated that coaching had a significant impact on at least one of nine business measures. In addition, they uncovered that overall productivity and employee satisfaction were the most positively impacted areas (which, in turn, have an impact on customer satisfaction, employee engagement, quality, annualized financial results, and more). In all, their study concluded that executive coaching produced a 788 percent ROI. The study noted that excluding the benefits from employee retention, a 529 percent ROI was produced.[16]

Manchester, Inc. surveyed one hundred executives, most of whom were from Fortune 1000 companies. Their research showed that a company's investment in executive coaching realized an average ROI of almost six times the cost of the coaching.[17]

According to the International Coaching Federation (ICF), 86 percent of organizations saw an ROI on their coaching engagements, and 96 percent of those who had an executive coach said they would repeat the process again.[18] Behind these results were tangible as well as intangible factors. Tangible factors were areas such as increased productivity, higher levels of overall employee performance, reduced costs, growth

---

16 Merrill C. Anderson, "Executive Briefing: Case Study on the ROI of Executive Coaching," MetrixGlobal, November 2, 2001, https://gvasuccess.com/articles/ExetutiveBriefing.pdf.

17 Joy McGovern et al. "Maximizing the Impact of Executive Coaching," *The Manchester Review* 6, no. 1 (2001): 3–11, https://www.perspect.ca/pdf/ExecutiveCoaching.pdf.

18 Simone Noordegraaf, "What Is Coaching, and What Makes It Such a Transformational Modality?," Institute for Professional Excellence in Coaching, November 21, 2019, https://www.ipeccoaching.com/blog/what-is-coaching.

in revenue and sales, higher employee retention, and higher engagement of employees. Intangible factors were increased confidence of those being coached, improved communication, and stronger employee, peer-to-peer, and key stakeholder relationships.

In their article, "How's Your Return on People?" Laurie Bassi and Daniel McMurrer note that three stock portfolios composed only of companies that "spend aggressively on employee development" each outperformed the S&P 500 by 17 to 35 percent during 2003.[19]

Other studies indicate positive ROIs as well, such as:[20]

- Improved executive productivity (reported by 53 percent of executives)
- Improvements in organizational strengths (48 percent)
- Gains in customer service (39 percent)
- Increased retention of executives (32 percent)
- Enhanced direct report/supervisor relationships (> 70 percent)
- Improved teamwork (67 percent)
- Improved peer-to-peer working relationships (63 percent)
- Great job satisfaction (52 percent)

Again, while much of this research is in the business world, it is intriguing to think what kinds of downstream benefits might be produced in a school and district if a concerted

---

[19] Laurie Bassi and Daniel McMurrer, "How's Your Return on People?," *Harvard Business Review*, March 2004, https://hbr.org/2004/03/hows-your-return-on-people.

[20] International Coach Federation and PricewaterhouseCoopers, *ICF Global Coaching Client Study* (International Coach Federation, 2009), https://www.michalholub.cz/download/ICF-Global-Coaching-Client-Study-complete.pdf.

effort to improve coaching and development of its leaders were to be made.

CONCLUSION

Let's go back to my airplane conversation with Michael Phelps. Albeit Phelps has the drive, motivation, and dedication to be an Olympian, he, too, has a coach. Michael Phelps's coach, Bob Bowman, played a pivotal role in shaping his legendary career. Bowman focused on long-term development, emphasizing hard work, discipline, and continuous improvement rather than just natural talent. He encouraged Phelps to embrace challenges and setbacks as opportunities for growth and used mental training techniques like visualization to build resilience. Bowman's tailored, individualized coaching helped Phelps develop both physically and mentally, enabling him to become the most successful swimmer in history through relentless dedication. "I knew what I needed to do," Phelps said, but he knew what he needed to do as an Olympian because Bowman helped coach him when he wasn't an Olympian.

So who is your Bowman? Who can turn challenges into opportunities? Who can say, "I know you're down today, but what can you do to get past that hurdle so you can continue to do what you want to do?"

If only good things result from the investment in good coaching, why don't educational leaders have trained coaches like everyone else? That's the question that has kept us up at night ever since we found coaches ourselves at the height of our educational leadership careers and wished we had them earlier.

The greatest in the world know they need a coach because

they know they're never done getting better. It seems ironic to us, then, that as educators steeped in the belief that our students can grow and change, the same can't be said for us.

Which leads us to the problem of change itself.

WORK SESSION 1: REFLECT TO FOCUS ON YOUR CURRENT REALITY

Principal Kiki stood in front of the faded map of Whitestone Elementary, a low-performing school in a struggling community. The school had been her responsibility for two years, and despite her relentless efforts, the needle hadn't moved much. Test scores were still below average, and teacher morale was low. Parents were losing faith in the school, and so was she. Kiki was finding it challenging to address Whitestone's unique needs.

Realizing she had been operating more as a manager than as a leader, Kiki was struggling with the transition to leading school improvement efforts. Her focus had been on day-to-day survival rather than implementing long-term systems and reflecting on strategies for progress. She felt unsure of how to move the school forward, particularly regarding negotiating with the teachers' union and engaging faculty and staff to support improvement goals. Although she was keen to build relationships and foster a positive environment, she was uncertain about the best approaches and how to drive change effectively. Aware that she could seek district support, Kiki struggled to put aside her imposter syndrome in fear that leadership would view her as a weak principal.

Key Actions and Reflections

School Leader Thought Work

- What are the similarities between my current situation and Principal Kiki's current situation?

- What are the differences between my current situation and Principal Kiki's current situation?
- What is in place to support my leadership capacity?

District Leader Thought Work

- What district-wide systems are in place to support principals who resemble Principal Kiki?
- What have I done to ensure school leaders feel comfortable coming to me for help?
- What district-wide systems are in place to support the growth of school leaders?

CHAPTER 2

Coaching Leads to Change

"Coaching school and district leaders to lead change means fostering a mindset that challenges old paradigms and creates new possibilities for learning and growth."

—Robert Hargrove, author

When Melinda became a new principal, she was quick to make changes. She noticed right off the bat that the teachers weren't being utilized effectively. The teachers were having the paraeducators take care of all recess duties while the teachers hung out in the lounge, apparently planning. Melinda made a quick fix. A lot of disciplinary infractions happened at recess because the students didn't have the same respect for the paraeducators' authority as they did for their regular teachers and were less likely to listen to their behavior redirects. So Melinda sent off a quick email that proclaimed the teachers were now going to be on recess duty with their classes and the paraeducators were to come inside and work with other grade levels during recess.

Boy, did *that* cause a rift. The teachers complained to the district, and soon the superintendent came to figure out what was wrong. The decision itself wasn't bad—it was still the right thing to do—but the process she took to implement it was seen as heavy-handed and arbitrary. She didn't communicate the problem she was attempting to solve and the way she wanted to solve it, and she didn't ask for the teachers' input and feedback as to how it would affect them or if there was a better solution.

We come up with an idea that we think will solve a problem, we try it, and a month later we're back in the same conference room looking at each other and wondering why it didn't work. And this failure occurs because, often, we didn't follow the change process.

Principals may have great insight and an inspirational vision to make beneficial changes to their school, but "when it comes to changing the world, what most of us lack is not the courage to change things, but the skill to do so."[21] Coaching is a powerful and highly effective way to help principals develop the skills and strategies necessary for making profound and lasting changes.[22] But while coaching is known to be an effective change strategy, we rarely use it in academic settings.

One common thread among failing schools is the lack of change management strategy among leaders. They'll get promoted, see the numbers, and yet keep everything the same, as if that is the answer to the problem. Which, of course, gets

---

21 Kerry Patterson et al., *Influencer: The Power to Change Anything* (McGraw Hill, 2008).

22 Robert Hargrove, *Masterful Coaching* (Wiley, 2008). Kindle.

them the same outcome as before: failure. "The coaching isn't working," they say. "Well, what have you tried to do?" we ask. And they can point to nothing in particular, except maybe a vague "worked on campus culture" or "smoothed out some operational duties." If you don't act and implement, of course you get the negative results you might anticipate if you are resistant to change: zero improvements.

> **IF YOU WANT THINGS TO CHANGE, YOU HAVE TO MAKE CHANGE—AND THAT CHANGE HAS TO BE DONE IN A WAY THAT STICKS.**

Which leads us to the question of which type of leader makes the most change, operational or instructional? That's where we will go next.

OPERATIONAL VERSUS INSTRUCTIONAL LEADERSHIP

When you first get promoted to principal, a whole host of responsibilities comes your way that you never thought of before, things like maintenance and budgets and payroll that have to do with how the campus functions and operates. If a new principal is coached by supervisors at all, advice pertaining to operations is normally what they get.

We used to jokingly refer to operational leadership as MBWA, or "management by walking around." As principals, we literally walked around and took care of things. This was the older model for how to do leadership at the school level. Our priorities were the things in front of our noses that we could see. Were our students happy? How was attendance?

Was there any new graffiti on the walls that needed to be painted over? If you were good at all those little things, then you ran a good school. Those were the days, way back in the early 1990s, when principals made regular trips to the classrooms just to say hello. They strove to learn all their teachers' names. All their students' names. All their students' parents' names. You sat in the lunchroom and chatted, having great conversations about the latest movie to come out or the culinary merits of burgers over pizza. You might have asked how the students' day was going, but as a leader you'd never dream of asking what they were learning. You rarely considered asking students about their data.

Now, we aren't saying relationship building isn't an important part of student success, and for teachers on the frontlines it can be the difference between one student passing or not. But at the campus level, for a principal responsible for the passing of all students, not just one, time and effort is better spent setting that teacher up for success so they have the knowledge and expertise to build those relationships more effectively in service to teaching and learning that ultimately drives school and student success.

The toilet broke in the third-floor girls' bathroom. Now I'm going to call someone to fix it and wait while they get here, then watch over their shoulder to make sure they're fixing it the right way, then check back in later to see if it's still fixed. A whole day for an operational principal could be spent focused on a toilet. Meanwhile, struggling teachers get punitive write-ups with cookie-cutter improvement plans that do nothing to actually help them become stronger teachers, and the students' grades are in the toilet.

Many principals still want to focus on culture. That's the fun part. The people part. It's the one you see face-to-face. It can make for a popular school, a fun school. We made our schools fun. Every Friday was movie day. Everyone wanted to go to our schools—but they weren't the best when it came to test scores and student learning outcomes.

But what we want to ask you now is this: Have you ever walked into a high-performing school with a bad culture and climate? So which comes first, culture or performance? The individual or the system? Or does creating a system where everyone can be successful, from teachers to staff to students, enable a healthy culture and climate to take root? Do you plant a nurtured seedling in a crummy field and expect it to grow up big and strong, or do you make for a healthy field that can support thousands of seedlings?

It is possible to create a school that feels good that is low performing. But if you focus on performance first and your school becomes high performing, guess what happens to culture and fun? They follow suit.

Culture and operations are not the drivers of instructional outcomes, the real purpose of schools. They support the learning environment, but they don't teach students subject matter. We also don't want to say they aren't important. However, as we've experienced ourselves, a school that feels good doesn't necessarily do good work. A positive culture and better maintenance alone are not going to improve test scores. We propose that prioritizing achievement drives cultural improvement, as data-driven gains in student outcomes foster a more positive and engaged school environment. It makes sense that people feel better when they are doing better.

As an instructional leader, you may not be spending as much time in the lunchroom, but the students still form relationships with their teachers when they visit them at lunch. And now the students talk to you about what they learn. They show you. Graphs and charts now line the third-grade hallway to show how students are progressing toward their goals. Assessments show how reading standards are improving for each student each semester and which students may need extra support. Collaborative meetings and norming sessions are held, where teachers weigh in on the current assessments and where they think they can help students improve or if they think the assessment itself can be improved. And if a teacher is struggling, there's a customized coaching plan in place to help that teacher grow their skills and give them the knowledge and support they need to move the needle on student outcomes. We talk about how to close the achievement gap on the standards that weren't mastered.

When Lorna was assistant principal, she loved handling discipline, talking to students to help them manage the problems that held them back. But when she became a principal, she was still doing discipline, even though that was now the job of her own assistant principal. For Melinda, her passion was supporting ELs and helping bilingual students succeed in English-speaking classrooms. She assigned herself to all the EL meetings, feeling she was the only one who could advocate for this student population. She could talk to the parents in Spanish to ensure these students were getting all the support they needed and the parents understood what was going on without anything being lost in translation.

But they each could have delegated those tasks to others with the time, ambition, and job scope to do them. They could have helped others develop through doing the jobs they loved while helping others get better.

You often have to let go of the daily tasks you love in order to love on a larger scale. Did Melinda want to impact tens of ELs or hundreds? Thousands? The question becomes how many people do you want to impact? The higher you go, the broader and bigger your impact. The more people you can reach. But that means also focusing on the bigger and broader systems that affect entire campuses and communities. Entire regions.

To be successful, we as leaders have to learn to adapt to change, just like any other leader. And then we have to turn around and teach others how to adapt to change so they can move forward with us.

If Lorna had wanted to keep doing discipline, she should have stayed in the assistant principal role because now all her time was taken up doing two jobs. She couldn't be in the classrooms focusing on instruction. She couldn't look at any data when she was doing discipline. When you change roles, you change goals. Accepting that priorities and job tasks will shift, become broader in scope, at higher levels is essential for success at those levels. Delegation becomes a friend, leaving the tasks that you loved behind to those now stepping into your old shoes…though don't forget to mentor those people, because to them they are new shoes, and maybe bigger shoes, to fill. And you'll find new loves in the new roles.

When someone goes from principal to district leader, they get promoted because they were a good principal, but they don't know what to do as a district leader. They didn't know what made them successful at lower levels of leadership, only that they were. You can't just take your case study of one and tell the next leader down the line, "Do what I did, and it will work out." That's a situational success, not a systemic success. That's an anecdote, not a best practice.

And we know this because it didn't even work for us. What worked in one context did not work in another. What worked in one school did not transfer over to the next. What worked at the school level did not work at the district level.

It's a move from a mindset of managerial operations to instructional leadership.

For an instructional leader, the focus shifts to "How can I support and elevate your instruction?" rather than discipline and spending duty in the lunchroom and operations. It's about empowering educators to refine their teaching practices, not just overseeing tasks.

And what about that toilet? Well, the toilet still gets fixed, now handled by a competent head custodian that knows to check it and how to proceed to fix it.

Relationships and toilets, while pieces of a school's success, do not determine a school's success. They don't necessarily transfer to high-performing schools.

There is a third type of leadership. It's been a buzzword in business circles for years but is relatively new to education. That's transformational leadership, or leadership that teaches people how to change. Because it's not enough to set up the systems, we also have to prepare people to adapt and use those systems as well as to take ownership of them and make them work for their situations. For example, if there's a system in place to account for and manage change, new student populations, new initiatives, new technology, new state laws, new assessments, everything that always and forever changes in schools and district, then we can create schools that not only perform well one year, but for decades into the future.

As leaders we can facilitate the hard process of change rather than force it, which, trust us, doesn't work. If people haven't bought into a change, they won't change, at least not for long. They'll resist at every step, becoming disgruntled and unhappy, and things will go back to the way they were the moment your back is turned.

So the next question is, what does sustainable change management look like in a school?

CHANGE MANAGEMENT IN EDUCATION

Lorna instituted teacher collaboration times at her middle school. Every Friday, the teachers for each grade level built curriculum together, such as common assessments and rubrics. It became a successful and popular program. When she was promoted to a high school, she declared her high school teachers would now be doing these collaboration times. Her pronouncement was met with blank stares and tight lips. "We know what we're doing," the teachers returned suspiciously. "Why do we have to meet and talk to each other?" Lorna was flabbergasted at the pushback. The middle school faculty had been all in from the beginning, seeing the value in the exercise. Lorna didn't know how to get buy-in to new programs, and she'd jumped with both feet into a crowded pool and wondered why everyone was upset when they got splashed.

Lorna's good idea failed when she took it to her new high school because she didn't understand change management. She thought it was a great idea. Her middle school teachers thought it was a great idea. She assumed her high school teachers would too. But these were different people, a different culture, and she hadn't yet earned their trust.

The Lorna of today would do things differently. She would recruit people interested in her new ideas. She would have given everyone the Why behind the change.

This brings us to another side to motivation that lies at the root of why many school leaders fail: they don't know how to change, and so they don't know how to change others.

Change management is leveraged in the business world,

with industry leaders touting all sorts of ways for companies to remain nimble and get people on board to create changes that are sustained even after the leaders that start them step down. That's the big dream of Maxwell's Level 5 of leadership, after all: you make a permanent change for the future and leave a positive impact. Successful leaders have a track record of being able to foster change successfully.

Just like other business strategies, change management has been slow to work its way into education administration, however, maybe because of the stigma of making education "businesslike," or because of the risk involved with change, or maybe because to champion change management, you have to have leaders who are open and capable of fostering change on broad scales.

If what you're doing isn't working, something needs to change.

To be clear, we don't want to turn schools into businesses. Public education and its mission to teach *all* students is in our blood. But we also know our effectiveness as education leaders, and our satisfaction with our jobs, improved drastically once we understood change management models. People are people, and the process works as well with districts and schools as it does with corporate employees.

Change is a risk, but as we who've been teachers tell our students, it's okay to take a risk, even as leaders. It's okay that we're not perfect the first time around, or that we make mistakes, or that an experiment we try fails. That's how we learn.

Businesses are ahead of the curve on accepting this risk and realizing that to make significant, lasting change, it has to be done methodically and systematically, accounting for everyone who has a stake in that change, who will be affected by it and who must implement, maintain, and assess its level of success.

Now, we could go on about change management in schools, and that may be a topic we take up in another book at another time. We don't have to be CEOs of nimble companies or presidents of universities to foster change. We can use change management to change systems to help better serve students in our schools too.

EFFECTIVE AND SUCCESSFUL CHANGE IS ONE OF THE GOALS AND UNIQUE CAPABILITIES OF COACHING.

COACHING LEADERS TO LEAD CHANGE

One of the urban districts in Texas near where we live recently passed a billion-dollar bond. The district used it to fix up all their schools. The buildings were beautiful. And then the district closed nineteen of them.

It seems that nobody thought through this change long term. No one looked at the root of the problem of low enrollment that prompted the schools to close. It obviously wasn't how the buildings looked.

When we each found coaching in our own paths to leadership, it was a revelation. "Where has coaching been all my life?" we thought. How different, how much better would we have been as leaders early on if we'd known how to go through those change management steps?

What coaching does powerfully is create a safe space for change, a zone free of the threat of reprisal or blame, and help show leaders how to coach and foster that change across their campuses and districts. As coaches, we facilitate the leaders we work with as they go through the steps of change to address the problems and people unique to their situation and school. Change is the path, and coaches are the guides along that path. But know that our ultimate goal is for those who first go along that path with us to become leaders who can then turn around and coach the next cohort of leaders along that path, and for the people they coach to become coaches in turn, creating a system of support within their own district and school that eventually takes care of itself.

Coaches help emerging leaders think through each step in the change process as the leaders identify what needs to be done to make change happen in their schools. Coaches are a mirror, a sounding board, a facilitator, or a phone-a-friend. We have the experience to play devil's advocate to see if the leader is thinking about all the angles and potential ramifications of a decision down the line. We can hold the big picture in our heads.

So far, coaching is the best, friendliest way we've found to change both ourselves and others to be more prepared, competent, effective, and, well, happy leaders ready to stick around for the tough battles schools always have to fight, through incredible obstacles, to help students learn better.

To be successful school and district leaders, we have to move away from spending buckets of money on the latest shiny initiative, lobbing it like a grenade into our school ecosystems, and then wondering why it blows up and doesn't work. It may not be the initiative that's at fault but the implementation of it: how we handle the change that initiative brings.

We know coaching is another shiny new thing, at least in academic circles, but the difference here is that coaching sets up a system to *help implement everything else.*

COACHING FACILITATES SUCCESS IN ALL AREAS BY CREATING A MECHANISM FOR CHANGE TO HAPPEN, WHATEVER THAT CHANGE IS.

To do anything takes a leader, even when it comes to deciding to be a leader at all.

CONCLUSION

To sum up, coaching plays a crucial role in effective leadership, particularly in guiding change. It equips leaders and their teams with the skills to navigate challenges and stay resilient, fostering flexibility and alignment toward shared goals. By creating a supportive environment, coaching encourages growth and innovation without fear of punishment. This makes coaching essential for leaders looking to inspire and successfully lead their teams through change.

Often as leaders we don't think we have time to dwell on what we believe deep down. We dive right in without even knowing, let alone be able to articulate, the nature of our character. By understanding where you stand, you'll be better equipped to leverage coaching continuous improvement.

The foundation of effective coaching begins with a thorough understanding of your current practices, strengths, and areas for improvement. The next chapters will guide you through a process of self-reflection and evaluation, defining and setting the stage for impactful coaching experiences. They'll help you answer the questions:

- What kind of leader am I?
- What do I value?

- How can my values be leveraged in my approach to leadership?
- Once I know who I am as a leader, how can I turn around and develop the leaders behind me?

To be a good coach, you must first know who you are and what you bring to the table. To coach others to their highest potential, you must first reach your own.

Let's start with Why.

WORK SESSION 2: IDENTIFYING BARRIERS TO CHANGE

Principal Kiki sat at her desk, surrounded by binders of school improvement plans and a growing to-do list. She felt the weight of Whitestone's challenges pressing on her: low staff morale, stagnant student outcomes, and mounting pressure from the district. But a spark of hope had emerged during a recent coaching session. Her leadership coach had asked a simple but powerful question: "What would strategic, lasting change look like for your school, and how will you lead it?"

That question stayed with her. Kiki realized that while she was constantly busy managing day-to-day issues, she hadn't yet carved out space to think and lead strategically. The idea of leading school improvement in a more intentional, focused way felt energizing but also overwhelming. Where would she start? How would she move from reacting to planning?

Instead of letting those questions swirl unanswered, Kiki made a choice. She scheduled a follow-up session with her coach and asked for support in mapping out a strategic improvement plan. Together, they could define key priorities, clarify "the Why" behind the change, and consider how to bring others along on the journey. It felt vulnerable to admit she didn't have it all figured out, but it also felt right.

As Kiki opened her laptop to start drafting some ideas before her coaching session, she felt a mix of determination and uncertainty. But for the first time in months, she also felt something else, a sense of direction and support. With the right guidance and a commitment to strategic leadership, she could begin building the foundation for real and sustainable change at Whitestone.

Key Actions and Reflections

School Leader Thought Work

- Reflect on Principal Kiki's scenario. What are the biggest barriers preventing you from shifting from "manager" to "strategic leader" in your own context?
- If you were to initiate a strategic improvement effort at your school, what priorities would you focus on first?
- What's one small, immediate action you could take this week, individually or with your coach, to begin leading change more intentionally?

District Leader Thought Work

- What challenges do principals in your district face when trying to lead strategic improvement instead of managing daily operations?
- If you were supporting Principal Kiki, what specific coaching structures, resources, or mindset shifts would help her build confidence and clarity?
- How can your district design systems that consistently support principals in thinking and acting strategically, not just reactively?

PART 2

Coaching Starts Within

CHAPTER 3

What Is Your Why?

"The two most important days in your life are the day you were born and the day you find out why."
—MARK TWAIN, AUTHOR

In the mid 1990s, Flip Flippen wrote *Capturing Kids' Hearts*,[23] a curriculum that inspired a nationwide professional development program focused on building strong relationships in education. One of the units focused on our stories, the Why behind our life's decisions.

Lorna was still a young principal when she took that training. She had to stand up and tell her story and the purpose it gave her in front of all the other participants. She couldn't do it. She didn't get it. "I went to college because my parents made me go to college," she said. True. She went to a four-year university after junior college, no degree plan, just thinking she needed a degree. In her junior year, her advisors sat her down. "What are you going to do?" They showed her

---

23 Flip Flippen, *Capturing Kids' Hearts* (The Flippen Group, 2005).

her transcript and added all the credits up with pencil and paper, and the closest degree she could finish in four years was elementary education. So she became a teacher.

Lorna didn't know her Why. There was obviously something there, or why else would she have taken all those education classes voluntarily? But as a young woman, she didn't know what it was, or why she liked those classes.

She participated in Trinity University's Principal Center in San Antonio and again encountered the by-now-infamous question: What is your Why? Finally, Lorna gave it some thought.

Now it all made sense.

She'd always worked in school districts with high poverty rates, similar to the school she had come from when she was young. Lorna realized she wanted to give her time to the toughest schools so she could give those students—who didn't have the kind of parental support and encouragement she had, who didn't know college admissions officers or possess a family history of higher education—the opportunity to see what a college degree could do for their future earning potential and social contributions. She did what she did so every child, no matter their home life or zip code or family income, had a chance at achieving their full potential.

"Why do you do what you do?" is the most important question for anyone, especially a leader hoping to be a coach, to answer. Otherwise, how are they going to help others discover what they themselves cannot? That's just Coaching (or Teaching) 101. So before any coaching can happen, the coach must first discover their own Why.

WHY YOUR WHY MATTERS

We can't discuss the concept of a Why without acknowledging Simon Sinek's *Start with Why: How Great Leaders Inspire Everyone to Take Action*. Sinek transformed leadership thinking by emphasizing purpose, visualized through his "Golden Circle" model. He argued that a leader's Why isn't about products or outcomes—it's the deeper reason behind their actions. When employees understand and connect with this purpose, it becomes embedded in the district and school's mission and vision. This alignment fosters buy-in across the organization, making it easier to navigate change as long as it stays true to that core Why.

You can't stop at defining Why; you have to define your Why in the context of your leadership and the high-performing teams you want to create. Your Why motivates and inspires the teams you build. To reach the core of Sinek's Golden Circle, reflect on key aspects of your purpose: the driving force behind your work, how it influences others, what it looks like in action, and how you empower others to discover their own Why to become effective leaders.

COACHING IS THE KEY TO LEADERSHIP SUCCESS IN EDUCATION.

Similarly to other professional spheres, coaching leads from the organizational level. The leader's focus shifts from fixing toilets to fixing the systemic issues that prevent students from reaching their highest potentials. Even as Melinda was elevated to positions such as assistant superintendent or CAO (chief academic officer), she always kept the coaching mentality she'd gained by doing group coaching sessions with her team. She'd bring in her direct reports for conversations to see what was going on at a broader level for them. How could she help?

Melinda's type of coaching encouraged her direct reports to think about the processes and systems that made their schools and districts function well. It resulted in better performance from her teams.

EDUCATION IS A SYSTEM; IT ISN'T A WHY. A WHY IS PERSONAL, INDIVIDUAL.

Many leaders, especially in schools, don't think too deeply about why they do what they do. "We do it for the students" is the standard answer. But that requires deeper understanding. It must reach the heart of every individual. We must be clear about what we are doing for students and what we want them to gain from us. Their experiences in our schools should leave a lasting impact, shaping their future beyond graduation. We don't know how many educators decided to become educators because of their own Why or if, like Lorna, they merely went through the motions and followed the path of least resistance.

We all get asked, "What do you want to be when you grow up?"

"I want to be a teacher."

Okay, why? What does being a teacher allow you to do? How does that role fill your cup?

And then you are a teacher, and someone taps you on the shoulder to become a school leader who maybe doesn't work with students every day. Well, what then? How does fixing toilets, balancing budgets, and having movie days "do it for the students"? What's behind the role? Why are you here?

Your Why is your personal mission and vision statement. The explanation of your purpose as a leader. Not the school's mission statement. Not the district's. Yours.

We all believe we're in our positions to make a difference for our students. But what is lacking in that blanket belief is each of our individual beliefs. We must all be able to answer the question "What can I do to help students succeed?" Often, this belief is tied to a big event in our own lives, a "disturbance in the Force," to quote Yoda, that drove us to pursue a career that, let's face it, often comes with more expectations and obstacles than we get paid to take on.

At the center of all this is that Why. It's the Why that keeps us going and keeps us in pursuit of our goals. When we lose sight of that Why, we have one foot out the door. Conversely, if we're forced to align to a district's Why that we as school leaders don't believe in, it may be time to part ways.

To start to build trust with the people you coach, you have to let them know what you stand for. Our personal life stories help people understand our stance on helping them be who they need to be to reach their full potential. That's the first step in building relationships and trust with those we coach.

But it isn't just beneficial to our role as coach for the people we want to help. It's also beneficial to us to know ourselves and what motivates us.

So how do we discover our Why?

Well, often it's hidden in our own stories.

THE POWER OF STORYTELLING

Melinda always liked kids, so teaching just seemed like a natural step along that path. What could be better than a career that centered around children? She thought the only thing she could do was get a degree in education because she'd be good at it. She didn't really think about *why* she was good with students or *why* she wanted to help them.

Years passed, and Melinda slowly climbed the leadership ladder, never delving too deeply into her reasons for doing so. Then people started to ask why she was there. They wanted her to connect her purpose to the school's vision of getting increased student success, or attendance rates, or civic engagement.

So Melinda had to take a long look at what her contributions were to these goals, and she found she always gravitated to equality and access for minority students and the line she never could forget from that long-ago guidance counselor, "You could be a good hairdresser," and her desire to reach children that looked like her. So Melinda discovered her Why: I can reach students just like me, who maybe haven't had a lot of educational support and encouragement along the way, and help them see how education can unlock doors to a bigger, better future. (If this Why sounds familiar, it is, because Lorna's is very similar—which may be why we work so well together.)

Melinda's story reveals another characteristic about our Why that we don't often think about. Identifying your purpose isn't so much finding a Why you don't yet have as it is uncovering something that was already there. The knowledge is already inherent in our stories; we just need a little help from a coach to pick out the pattern.

Reflect on your story within your institution—how you

arrived, the leader you aspire to be, and how you invite others to engage with your journey. Define your personal vision for the future and share your story with intention. Seek feedback, incorporate it into your evolving narrative, and, most importantly, create a supportive space for others to share their own stories.

Stories trigger our empathy. They give us credibility. They show we have lived it, felt it, done it. And yes, sometimes failed, just like normal humans do. They promote a feeling of family, *la familia*, that we're all in this together. If someone knows who you truly are and what you stand for, they are more willing to advocate for you.

Stories encourage you to think about who you are in this organization and mission with others. This builds high-performing teams in your organizations because people can see you for who you are. The facade is down. This is where I came from. This is who I am. This is what I believe.

Many people assume others will pick up on their story because it's so obvious. This is far from true. Stories that aren't spoken create an environment of stories in our heads. If you don't tell your story, people invent stories about you. That story will most likely be wrong, and you'll have no idea what that story is, but it will become the basis for why people don't trust you or want to have a relationship with you.

Lorna once had a teacher who stood in the hallway during passing and yelled at students. Every day, she'd be out there snapping at students to hurry, to get to class, to tuck their shirts in, to watch what they were doing. One day, Lorna brought this teacher into her office. "The story in my head," she said bluntly, "is that you don't like students."

The teacher gasped in surprise. "Why would you think that?"

Lorna looked at her pointedly. "Because you stand in the hallway and yell at them all day."

Then the teacher burst into tears. "My God, I love students. I raise my voice because I want them to be so much better. I'm hoping they'll finally hear me."

Lorna sat back. The old story in her head was now completely gone. "Well, if that's the case, let's figure out a better way to get them to listen to you than yelling."

Before this conversation, Lorna was about to coach this teacher out of teaching. Now, knowing more of her story, that approach changed to giving her more effective communication tools that helped both her and her students move forward. The teacher's external behavior now more closely matched her internal story.

Everybody has a story in their head because that's how humans think. Each of us is made up of not one story but hundreds. Thousands. All of which contributed in some fashion to who we are today and why we do what we do. But if we don't tell them, someone else will. If we don't shape the narrative, others will create one in our place. So take control over your own story and tell it like you want it to be told, even if it hurts.

As a principal, Melinda had an amazing second-grade teacher at a little Title I campus. Dynamic and kind, a veteran teacher of over a decade, she had a 90 percent pass rate. At every collaborative meeting, Melinda tried to get this teacher to share her teaching techniques, but at this prompting, the teacher always shut down and went quiet.

Finally, Melinda got so frustrated with this teacher's lack of participation that she held the teacher back after one of the collaborative meetings and lectured her on the importance of sharing teaching strategies. "Everyone works together here,"

Melinda huffed. "Why aren't you willing to share what you are doing?"

The teacher shuffled her feet and looked at the ground. "Because I'm embarrassed," she said. "Growing up, anytime I'd share with my siblings, they would all attack me. They'd make me feel like what I said wasn't worth anything."

Melinda was taken aback. She realized that every time she asked this teacher to share, she was inadvertently taking her back to a dark place Melinda hadn't even known existed. The story in her head, that this teacher was a super-confident whiz, hadn't helped anyone.

From then on, instead of calling this teacher on the carpet, Melinda worked with her before these meetings. They practiced her responses. Melinda gave her stem sentences and prompts she could answer and take notes on days before the next collaborative meeting. Eventually, with much gentle encouragement, practice, and newfound confidence, this teacher became a perfect mentor for new teachers.

Now, for this particular coaching journey to work, the teacher had to first take the plunge and be vulnerable with her principal, which we admit is hard to do. It's even harder for a leader to get vulnerable with their faculty and staff, those they are supposed to be leading.

However, to be a good leadership coach and find empathy for your coachee, you must be willing to reveal your mistakes and vulnerabilities. You don't necessarily have to reveal the darkest places of your past, but you at least have to recognize when you didn't know as much as you do now.

It's another kind of mindset, a reflective mindset that allows you to know yourself well enough to be able to coach others. Sometimes we look back on our leadership experiences and recognize moments of being coached only in hindsight. We didn't think that question or bit of advice that shifted our worldview was coaching. We didn't call it that. We thought they were just giving advice.

IT TAKES VULNERABILITY TO ACCEPT WHEN WE NEED TO MAKE A CHANGE AND GROW AS A LEADER.

But no change happens when people are comfortable. It takes a little bit of pain, a new idea that shows the old idea is too limited, to prompt new thinking and innovation. A desire to do better.

As a high school principal, Lorna used to stand at the front door of her school every day, and when the students were late, she'd bark, "Hurry up, you're late!"

One day, a kid walked through the door, trailing behind the others, shoulders hunched, and Lorna snapped her normal, "You're late!"

The kid gave her a quick, solemn look. "But I came."

Three little words, and Lorna felt the earth shift a little under her feet. What was the story behind that bitter, short sentence? Lorna didn't know, but she didn't have to know to act on it.

From that day on, Lorna stood at the door and said something different. "I'm so happy you're here today! Let's hurry up and get to class because it's already started." She made a change because that one fleeting glance into that student's life reframed how Lorna thought of the entire student population and the reasons why they might not get to school on time.

Stories can protect you from losing your Why. To paraphrase an old proverb, "If you don't stand for something, you'll fall for anything." Supporting students who'd had a hard-knock life was Lorna's Why, even if at the time of this incident she didn't know it. Her internal story made her rethink her approach to her students and how she needed to respond to them to remain true to that Why.

Stories provide the emotional charge that gets people to care about making a change. Something has to happen to trigger change, and most of us don't change based on abstract hypotheticals. We change because we met one person whose story made us see the status quo isn't working for everyone and remaining the same instead of making a difference leads to real-life consequences—which is really why we're all here, right? To make a difference. To change it up. To leave a young life better than we found it.

IF YOU WANT TO TRANSFORM SCHOOLS, SHARE THE STORIES THAT BUILD THE RELATIONSHIPS THAT CATALYZE TRANSFORMATION.

CONCLUSION

If we had not had the experience of discovering our Whys amid the jumble of our own stories, we wouldn't be coaches. Training alone does not make wonderful coaches. A certification does not guarantee success. For us, it was the activities and experiential learning that made us effective.

Sharing stories gives credibility to both the coach and the coachee and helps build an empathetic relationship. Coaching can help draw out the stories that need to be told for everyone to grow: the stories of who we were, who we are now, and what we can become.

Being authentic and vulnerable, knowing your own Why, is necessary to connect with others. It is your first superpower to be successful in coaching.

Once you uncover your Why, it's time to examine your beliefs, values, and behaviors around that Why. What action does your Why inspire?

WORK SESSION 3: CREATING AND COMMUNICATING YOUR WHY

Principal Kiki was at a family function over the holiday break when her cousin asked how she was enjoying her role as a school leader. Overwhelmed, Kiki broke down in tears, revealing her struggles and feelings of inadequacy. Her cousin suggested she might consider quitting and finding a different career. As Kiki caught her breath, she had a profound realization: she didn't want to leave her role. Her passion had always been to make a difference in the lives of students and teachers. Coming from a family that emphasized the importance of bettering oneself through education, she wondered why her passion for education wouldn't allow her to walk away.

Principal Kiki decided to take a step back and give herself the space to reflect. That weekend, she retreated to a quiet spot in the nearby hills, away from the noise of the school and the pressures of her role. She took a notebook and began to write, asking herself a simple question: Why did I become a principal?

She thought back to her early days as a teacher, where she had seen the impact of caring, individualized attention on her students. She remembered the joy of seeing a child's eyes light up when they finally grasped a difficult concept. She believed in education as a tool for empowerment, a way to break the cycle of poverty and open doors to a better future.

Key Actions and Reflections

School Leader Thought Work

- Think back to the moment or series of events that led you to pursue leadership in education. What was the driving force? What inspired you to become a school or district leader?
- Why do you believe your work as a school or district leader is important? Articulate the deeper purpose behind your efforts. How does your work contribute to the broader goals of education and society?
- If you could focus on one aspect of your role that aligns most with your Why, what would it be? Identify the area where you feel most passionate and impactful. How can you prioritize this in your daily work?
- How are you going to ensure your Why remains at the center of your leadership journey? Consider strategies to keep your purpose front and center. How can you align your actions, goals, and decisions with your Why?

District Leader Thought Work

- What inspired you to take on a leadership role within the district? Consider your motivations and how they align with the district's mission. How does this inspire your work in supporting school leaders?
- How do you ensure that the principals you oversee remain connected to their Why in their leadership journey? Reflect on the systems and practices in place that help school leaders stay aligned with their core motivations and purposes.
- How does the district support principals in focusing on areas of their role that align most with their Why? Identify how district policies, professional development, and resources are designed to empower principals to work in areas where they are most passionate and impactful.

CHAPTER 4

Beliefs, Values, and Behaviors

"Leadership is not about titles or the corner office. It's about the willingness to step up, put yourself out there, and lean into courage. The world is desperate for braver leaders. It's time for all of us to step up."

—Brené Brown, *Dare to Lead*

For Melinda, going from teacher to school and district leader to coach and consultant was always a process of growth. As a principal, she was a novice, naive about what it was she needed to do or how she needed to lead. Whatever goals she was given by her supervisors, she would work toward.

But Melinda didn't understand how important coaching could be to bringing about change that was sustained. She merely managed the people under her, telling them what to do and how to do it. She did what other people told her to do because of what they believed was important, but she didn't know why those goals or the actions she took to accomplish them were important to her.

Melinda will tell you that the biggest reason she lacked understanding was because she lacked not only her Why but the knowledge of her own beliefs, values, and behaviors (BVBs) that underpinned that Why.

Leaders don't normally examine their own BVBs, but they impact a leader's effectiveness since BVBs help us become our authentic selves. The way you show up is driven by your BVBs, and it is useful to know how your BVBs inform your feelings and responses to others. Once you know your authentic self, you are not only more confident in why and how you want to do this work, but that authenticity starts building trust in your coachees so they feel comfortable becoming authentic themselves.

Coachees don't know what they don't know in terms of skills. But somewhere inside, they do know what they believe and value, though they may not recognize when those internal thoughts manifest in their work. Part of a coach's job is to make the invisible visible for those they lead and coach. And if you want to be a good leader and coach, you have to first do the work you're going to be asking your staff and coachees to do.

DEFINING BELIEFS, VALUES, AND BEHAVIORS

One of Melinda's core values is accountability. Her mother always held Melinda and her siblings accountable for everything, including cleaning house, grades, choices in boyfriends, and going to college (which was nonnegotiable). For Melinda, if you say you're going to do something, she expects you to take ownership of that task and do it. She's not sure where this particular value came from, but she knows it permeates all her interactions. Everybody that's dear to her is held accountable for their actions or lack thereof, including her own daughter. Sometimes this value causes strains in Melinda's relationships because she finds herself being hard on people when the results of their actions do not meet expectations.

Melinda's value of accountability drives the actions and behaviors she takes with others, but that value did not come out of nowhere. Values do not manifest out of a vacuum. They come from our beliefs.

Beliefs are your assumptions about what is true. This is your personal operating system, coded into your brain by a bit of biology and a healthy dose of cultural and institutional knowledge passed on by your family, church, community, and, yes, school. Beliefs also come from chosen social groups, such as sports leagues, clubs, and social media. They coalesce from these sources of information and influence to become part of your personality and identity. They may shift over time with new information and experiences, but this usually happens slowly, and it can't be forced upon someone from the outside. Someone can fake believing what others believe, such as "liking" pepperoni pizza because everyone else says they like pepperoni pizza, but their heart will not change unless they want it to. Inside, they will still hate pepperoni pizza and pine for the Hawaiian pizza everyone says is uncool. In another example, you believe everyone should be accountable for their actions and deliver high standards because you yourself were expected to surpass your parents and be accountable for managing your own success, like Melinda.

Values form from beliefs. These values then set your moral compass. They are the abstract principles that guide concrete behaviors. Lorna's belief in a fair shot for at-risk students means she values equity. Therefore, her actions focus on equity-driven goals, such as ensuring access to rigorous curriculum for all students, providing targeted instructional coaching for teachers, or implementing data-driven interventions to close achievement gaps.

We often get asked in workshops, when we challenge people to define their values, whether we mean values "at home or at work." But the truth is, no matter which role or place you occupy, *your values are the same.* Melinda values accountability both at home and at work. Lorna values access to fair opportunities for her family, friends, and students. The actions and behaviors may change from context to context, but the values that drive them don't.

Values, *all* our values, impact learning outcomes. Here's a thought exercise that may help you see what we mean. We'll use the old adage "I believe all children can learn." Now really look at that belief. *Do* you believe *all* children can learn? Do you believe EL students can learn? What about special needs students? Students with behavioral issues? Students who are poor, or who have one parent, or who are sports stars? Take actions that *show* you believe all these groups can learn. Help each group's specific learning needs and challenges to set them up for success.

Beliefs, values, and the behaviors that follow from them are who you are. If you don't believe a certain group of students can learn, they won't learn. Students can sense words that are inauthentic, especially if those words are paired with curriculum and policies and supports (or lack thereof) that hinder more than help them. To be effective leaders, we must acknowledge that we carry many values and beliefs, some of which might even contradict each other, especially when it comes to different levels of leadership. For a quick example, district leaders care a lot about budgets. They have to keep the school solvent. But keeping budgets in line might mean cutting paraeducators and support staff for EL students or students with disabilities, which, necessary or not, communicates particular messages.

Students rise to the level of our expectations. Teachers know this. But sometimes school leaders forget this fact or don't realize what lies at its heart. Students don't succeed to get a high score on a standardized test and get the school a good state grade. Students graduate from high school because someone believed in them, more than any other factor. They succeed because they found someone whose beliefs and values aligned with their own.

As important as they are, beliefs and values often get short shrift when it comes to what people actually pay attention to.

Not to consciously adopt a metaphor from *Shrek*, but, pretend you're an onion. In the middle of that onion are your values. Unlike a real onion, we can't cut you open to see your values, but they are there nonetheless, under layers of lived experience. These core values affect your attitudes toward new information, which then affect your responses and behaviors. The behaviors, all the way on the outside of the onion, are what we can see. Even for ourselves, we pay more attention to the actions we take than to the values that drive them at our core. Values, like our beliefs, are so much a part of us they often go unnamed and unexamined.

Like our onion, people don't see your core values; they see your behaviors. They can guess at your values, but they may guess wrong—have that wrong story in their heads.

Behavior reflects words. Behaviors, what you see of the onion, indicate what values you think are important.

For instance, Lorna coached a principal with over five

years of experience who considered herself to be hands-on. The district had done a ton of work promoting collaborative meetings. Two months rolled by. The principal was proud of her collaborative meetings. She insisted on the importance of collaborative meetings. She was pushing collaborative meetings with her faculty. "Great," Lorna said. "How many collaborative meetings have you sat in on this year?"

"Zero," the principal admitted.

"What does that behavior show to your staff?" Lorna challenged.

"That I don't think collaborative meetings are important?"

Bingo.

Ask your colleagues, not your friends or family, as they know you too well, what they think your values are based on your behaviors and actions. If they say something that does not sound like you, then your behaviors need to change to more obviously reflect your values.

When we look at a leader and what they offer, we see their credentials. We see their skills. We see their education. But when we think about coaching leaders, we have to go below the tip of the iceberg to get a handle on the full depth of emotions, beliefs, and motivations underlying those competencies: Here's who I am. Now how do I connect that to my leadership style? To the work that I do with my coachees, staff, and students?

THE ROLE OF CHARACTER AND VIRTUES IN COACHING AND INSTRUCTIONAL LEADERSHIP

Effective coaching and instructional leadership go beyond strategies and skill building; they are deeply rooted in character and virtues. A leader's beliefs and values shape their decisions, influence their interactions, and ultimately define the culture they create. Without strong character, leadership becomes transactional rather than transformational.

AT THE CORE OF GREAT COACHING IS INTEGRITY, THE ALIGNMENT OF BELIEFS, VALUES, AND ACTIONS.

Coaches and instructional leaders must model honesty, fairness, and accountability to build trust with educators. When leaders consistently act with integrity, they create an environment where teachers and staff feel safe to grow, reflect, and take risks in their practice.

One of the things many certified coaches must abide by are professional certified coach (PCC) markers, such as maintaining confidentiality, trust, and ethical practices. All of these competencies make up a coach's character. A coach must cultivate trust and safety in the coaching relationship, ensuring that the coach's biases take a back seat and don't color the coachee's choices. Coaches embrace diverse perspectives.

So how do a coach's ethics, integrity, conduct, and values connect to form their character? Having good character means having good ethics, which creates safe and open spaces to be vulnerable and share without the coachee (or coach!) feeling like confidentiality will be broken if some sort of embarrassing mistake is revealed.

Solid, authentic relationships can't be faked. There is no "I only like you when I coach you." The relationship goes beyond the bounds of the conference room. And this kind of leadership by character, where people want to make you proud and celebrate their wins with you because they feel like you care about those wins, goes a long way to motivate a more reluctant coachee.

A coach treats every individual with respect and fairness so that they can have access to a successful coaching program regardless of their personal or professional background or circumstances. Whether they were chosen to have a coach through direct impact or got an opportunity to sign up for a coaching program under their own volition, we want the coachee to remain true to themselves.

To do this, as a coach, think about the coachee's individual needs. What barriers does the coachee face that you don't? This will help you remain compassionate and open to the coachee's perspective and more willing to give them the benefit of the doubt even when you disagree with them. This creates the positive environment that is essential for establishing trust and for viewing marginalized and struggling groups within the school and district with a growth mindset.

The strongest leaders are those whose beliefs and values drive their actions. They are not just managing teams or implementing initiatives; they are shaping the future of education by ensuring that every student, regardless of background, has access to high-quality learning experiences. By leading with character, instructional leaders inspire others to do the same, creating lasting change in schools and beyond.

EVERYONE'S BELIEFS ARE VALID

When Melinda begins a coaching relationship now, she starts by sharing her own beliefs. "I'm a first-generation Mexican American. That background founded my belief system. It comes with its own traditions and value structures. It dictates my behaviors toward the world around me. I must be aware of how my identities shape my biases and preferences, and others must know that this is where I come from. I must always work to neutralize my biases by taking a step back from the responses of the people I coach, knowing their beliefs, values, and behaviors come from a different background and they may not match my own."

It sounds a little like a mantra, because it is, or should be, for every leader and coach. Once a coach is able to embrace and accept their beliefs, values, and behaviors and the biases and emotions that come with them, that coach can consciously choose to set them aside and instead make the session about what the coachee's beliefs, values, and behaviors are and how they can be aligned better to grow the coachee into a better leader.

As coaches, we start getting below the surface to see the full iceberg by having a conversation about BVBs up front.

1. This is who I am.
2. This is what I believe.
3. This is how I like to coach.
4. Now, who are you?
5. What do you believe?
6. How do you like to be coached?

As coaches, we want to know the BVBs of our coachees so we can ensure that we support their own value system so they can grow. And we want them to know ours to avoid any of those sabotaging stories in the head and so they know up front that even though our backgrounds may be different, we think everyone's BVBs are valid.

So when we coach others, we start with our most important question: "What do you really believe?" Then we perform our most important action: we don't reject the answer.

ANYBODY CAN BE COACHED SO LONG AS THEIR VALUES AND BELIEFS ARE VALIDATED.

Beliefs and values are often what people protect at all costs, whether they understand that they are doing so or not, and this is where resistance to coaching can enter the picture, if the coachee feels that the coach does not know or understand their beliefs or take them seriously.

Therefore, when building a coaching relationship with a coachee, beliefs, values, and behaviors (BVBs) must be validated. They don't have to be best practices, but they do have to be respected. And woe to the leader who forces their values onto others.

Lorna's core value as a principal was to help every kid that came through the door. Literally, she'd register whoever needed a school to go to. "We'll figure something out," she'd say. In her middle school, with a good support system in place for at-risk students, acting on this value worked. But because Lorna didn't know how, exactly, her middle school's organically produced support system came to be, she had a hard time repeating this support system when she moved to a high school.

The edict to "register every student" ended up creating a rift between Lorna and her faculty, as more and more students who'd failed out of other high schools ended up at her high school's doors because "they took everybody." Without a system in place to support those struggling students' needs, they invariably failed in Lorna's school, too, as the teachers struggled to fulfill needs they didn't feel equipped to meet.

But Lorna didn't put all the pieces together. She didn't understand why everyone wouldn't want to help every student that walked through the door. She'd never been coached to examine her own values and how they showed up in her decisions. And she certainly didn't think about asking her teachers about their values!

Lorna knew she stood for students' opportunity to learn. If you didn't agree with her wholeheartedly, like some of her teachers, well, Lorna wasn't hearing it. She became very judgmental. She was already competitive (another of her values) and saw things as either win or lose, good or bad, right or wrong. If you didn't agree with her, then you were against her. If you didn't want to play on her team, you could find another.

This attitude, of course, was not going to help Lorna help her teachers help students. She didn't know it at the time, but she had a long way to go in terms of opening her mind to her beliefs, values, and behaviors and how they affected others through her actions.

When we get a response or idea we don't like or agree with, the natural impulse is to interject our own beliefs and values into the conversation: "Your way is wrong; my way is right, so you should do it my way." That's how top-down management often works.

However, the job of a coach is to go from the ground up. "What is your way? How is it working out for you?" For the people we coach, often the first response is pushback to any of our suggestions: "I don't think that's the best way to do it." But over time, with gentle pressure, a gentle insistence to identify the proof that their way is getting the hard results their state or district is telling them they need, a coachee willing to listen to the evidence shifts to be open to other solutions.

Part of this shift, as we've noted before, comes from allowing the coachee to be vulnerable and admit a gap in knowledge or skill. We want a coachee to say, "Wow, I didn't know that! Let's try it," rather than be in a state of silent or not-so-silent defensiveness where every weakness and area of ignorance is hidden from potential enemies out to reprimand them or remove them from their job.

Ethics can be right and wrong. It's wrong to cheat. It's right to give every student a chance. But as far as beliefs and values go, and the way you see the world, there is only meeting people where they are at and coaching them up to be better versions of themselves. Who are we to tell you your values are wrong?

As coaches, we don't want you to feel you are wrong—at least, not coming from us—but we do hope you'll have a moment where you see that no one else is wrong either. That you can step into someone else's shoes to see where they are coming from and why they believe and value what they do. To get to know them and meet them halfway.

If you come in with a mindset that everyone is wrong but you, there is no chance for the other person to grow. They won't trust you. Beliefs are the most precious part of us. To invalidate them is to invalidate a person's identity. People only truly change and grow if the change comes from themselves.

If you are coaching, it is important to know what you believe and value and how you behave, as much as it's important to know the BVBs of your coachee. You coach around the coachee's values, not around your own. You don't want to impose your values as a coach on your coachee.

As a coach, it's important to show up ready and able to listen to and accept someone else's truth. Only once that truth is acknowledged and centered as the motivator for future plans and actions can coaching be effective in doing the job it's meant to do: facilitating growth and change.

SYSTEM OF SUPPORT

One of Melinda's former coachees had been out of the public school system for over ten years. At the behest of district leaders, he'd come back to help a school turn around a dysfunctional campus culture. When Melinda met him, he had been asked to reduce staffing to make up a six-figure budget shortfall. He didn't use seniority to decide who would go. He chose the ones he felt weren't contributing to the environment he wanted. The hard decision had left him in the doldrums. He'd only been back to work three weeks, and all he'd done was work to repair trust and relationships.

Melinda knew the next step was to focus on work that had to be done, namely a plan that would support the school despite the decreased staffing.

How could she guide this principal to think beyond relationships and focus on the connection between expectations, results, and beliefs? He firmly believed that if his staff got along, they would naturally do the right thing to improve student success. But was camaraderie alone enough to drive instructional improvement and measurable outcomes?

This is where coaching can introduce the "yes/but" sentence template to challenge assumptions and encourage deeper reflection. "Yes, you believe they'll do the right thing if they get along, but how does that support your own belief system?" By posing this question, she nudged the principal to examine whether trust and collaboration, while valuable, were sufficient to ensure accountability and growth.

His response was immediate: "Just because it's my belief doesn't mean it's everybody else's belief." That moment of realization opened the door for a more structured conversation.

"So what's the system you have to create that supports both your beliefs as a leader and your staff's beliefs about student improvement? How will your teachers be held accountable for student success?" she prompted. The question wasn't just about reaffirming his belief in positive relationships; it was about translating that belief into action through systems, structures, and clear expectations.

The principal's honest response of "I don't know" set the stage for the next cycle of coaching. This uncertainty wasn't a setback; it was an opportunity. It signaled the need to codevelop a plan that balanced trust with accountability, ensuring that the belief in collaboration didn't overshadow the responsibility to produce results.

Melinda encouraged the principal to reflect not only on his beliefs but also on how those beliefs translated into expectations and results. He shared his conviction that if his staff could simply get along, collective goodwill would naturally lead to better outcomes for students. But Melinda challenged him to go deeper. "Is shared harmony enough to drive meaningful change?" This prompted a new line of thinking, one that moved from personal belief to organizational behavior.

Once values are identified, they are actionable, both at the personal and organizational level. But what if there's no action? If you have a belief, and it shows up in your policies and practices, there has to also be a system to support it.

Effective leadership requires building systems that set teachers up for success. Holding teachers accountable for student achievement means establishing clear expectations, firm timelines, and measurable criteria. Leaders must define what success looks like in practice and ensure that structures like assignment instructions, rubrics, outcomes, and due dates are in place. The same accountability systems that support students also support teachers.

If a principal values student success, they might implement

collaborative meetings to drive improvement. If those meetings don't produce results, the leader must assess whether the system needs refinement or better implementation. Too often, leaders blame teachers for not using a tool correctly instead of evaluating whether the training or support provided was sufficient. Is it the rod that's at fault, the fisherman, or the one who taught the fisherman to fish?

True coaching fosters growth, not exit strategies. Leaders must believe in their team's ability to improve. Providing a tool isn't enough; ongoing guidance and reinforcement are necessary. Moving a school forward means identifying gaps in the system rather than placing blame. Growth happens when expectations are clear, support is in place, and every educator is given the opportunity to succeed.

CONCLUSION

To lead and coach effectively, you must first understand who you are. Leading with integrity means staying grounded in your values and character, even in the face of challenge or change. Coaching others requires that same level of self-awareness, honoring your own beliefs, values, and behaviors (BVBs) while also creating space to understand and respect the BVBs of those you support. This balance is at the heart of authentic, transformative leadership. Knowing where you stand also allows you to consciously set that information aside so you can concentrate on helping others know themselves. The mind opens to curiosity and creativity, kindness and compassion. Dare we say even love?

And it is this self-knowledge and love of who we are and who others are that lays the foundation for the coaching mindset.

WORK SESSION 4: IDENTIFYING BELIEFS, VALUES, AND BEHAVIORS

One evening, after another long day, Principal Kiki sat alone in her office. She stared at the school's mission statement on the wall: "To empower every student to reach their full potential." The words felt hollow, disconnected from the reality of the school's struggles. She realized that she had been so focused on fixing problems that she hadn't stopped to reflect on what her core values and beliefs were as a leader.

Principal Kiki believed in the power of community, knowing that a school's success depended on the strength of its connections with families and the neighborhood. Most importantly, she believed in resilience, or the idea that even in the face of great challenges, both students and staff could overcome obstacles with the right support.

But Principal Kiki wondered what her values really were and if she had lost sight of her values in the daily grind of managing a struggling school. She had become so focused on metrics and mandates that she had forgotten to lead with her heart. She had been trying to solve problems without first grounding herself in what she truly believed. But as she sat in her office, grappling with these thoughts, the question loomed larger in her mind: What should she do next? The answer wasn't clear, and the path forward felt more uncertain than ever. Principal Kiki took a deep breath, knowing that whatever decision she made would define not just her career but the future of the school she had vowed to lead.

And with that, she knew it was time to make a choice.

Key Actions and Reflections

School Leader Thought Work

- List the top three to five values that are most important to you as a school leader (e.g., integrity, equity, respect, innovation, accountability). For each value, briefly explain why it is significant to you.

- How do your values align with your school's mission and vision? Analyze the connection between your personal values and the overarching goals of your school. Are there any gaps?
- In what ways do you model these values for your staff and students? Consider specific actions or behaviors that demonstrate your commitment to your values.
- What legacy do you hope to leave behind in your school community? Think about the long-term impact you want to have. How do you want to be remembered by your colleagues, students, and the community?

District Leader Thought Work

- List the top three to five values that are most important to you as a school leader (e.g., integrity, equity, respect, innovation, accountability). For each value, briefly explain why it is significant to you.
- How do your values align with your school's mission and vision? Analyze the connection between your personal values and the overarching goals of your school. Are there any gaps?
- In what ways do you model these values for your staff and students? Consider specific actions or behaviors that demonstrate your commitment to your values.
- What legacy do you hope to leave behind in your school community? Think about the long-term impact you want to have. How do you want to be remembered by your colleagues, students, and the community?

CHAPTER 5

The Coaching Mindset

"Before you tell me how to do it better, before you lay out your big plans for changing, fixing and improving me, before you teach me how to pick myself up and dust myself off so that I can be shiny and successful—know this: I've heard it before. I've been graded, rated and ranked. Coached, screened and scored. I've been picked first, picked last and not picked at all. That was just KINDERGARTEN."

—DOUGLAS STONE, *THANKS FOR THE FEEDBACK*

Now that you've identified your Why and BVBs, you have a good idea of who you are, where you come from, and what motivates you as a coach. You know what you love, but how do you adapt what you love to help someone else? How do you turn your attention to the people you are going to coach?

Like with lesson planning and preparation to teach in a classroom, coaching takes both planning and preparation. You can plan a huge, beautiful dinner. Eight courses, including dessert. But if you don't prepare the dinner after you plan it, nobody's going to eat, right? Planning maps out what you are going to do, the big picture topics you want to hit. Preparation is getting the documents, questions, and activities together and organizing schedules and meeting places. You can't just plan; you have to prepare.

And that includes preparing mentally to coach.

Before stepping into your first session with your coachee, it's important to get into the mindset of a coach. Starting off on the right foot with a positive connection makes the rest of the coaching process a whole lot easier and much more impactful and pleasant for everyone.

A successful coaching relationship allows both you and your coachee to get the most benefit out of your time and effort together. Here's how to prepare your mindset for that relationship.

AUTHENTIC COACHING

When we hire coaches, they don't often come in with extensive coaching experience. They are successful school and district leaders who have transformed schools. They can lead but do not always know how to coach. They know how to plan, and they know how to learn. But they don't know what they don't know about the practice of coaching. At first, they fall back on what they know already about transmitting personal experience and knowledge.

To provide a visual, Carmen is a district leader with a half dozen school leaders she coaches. She prepared a fabulous PowerPoint presentation with beautiful graphics to review with her coachees. But while the presentation looked beautiful, it meant Carmen did all the talking, and it was the same presentation material for all her coachees.

Caleb's coaching sessions primarily centered on his coachees reading a number of books on how to be better principals. While Caleb isn't doing the talking himself, he's delegating out the advice and lecture-giving to books. Again, the planning for each coaching session is the same no matter who the coachee is.

Martin, a former superintendent, had all the answers. His sessions consisted of a lot of sentences that started with "Don't do that" and "You should do this."

These coaching sessions were all about advising and telling, not coaching.

Telling and advising forms a teacher-student relationship, something many beginner coaches are familiar with from working with students. But the teacher-student relationship doesn't work the best when we want a coachee to (1) feel they are on the same level of authority with their coach, (2) articulate their own goals, and (3) figure out how to meet those goals with the knowledge and tools they have available.

A leadership coach is different, again, than the concept of "coach" we as educators are familiar with from school sports. A football or basketball coach *does* tell and advise. They have to. Their players don't yet know the game or the safe and effective ways to play it. Sports coaches are more like teachers than the coaches that serve business and industry leaders.

As coaches to school and district leaders, we must occupy a role more akin to those business coaches. We want to coach better leaders who think for themselves, not just performers who execute what they are told to do without thinking about the reasons or ramifications of what they are doing.

Our coachees already know a lot. They're smart and credentialed and have been successful in other roles—that's why they were selected to be leaders. So these leader-coachees must be approached as equals who need someone to shine a light on what they don't know, both in terms of problems and solutions. They can then choose to take up what's illuminated and use and adapt it how they see fit.

Coaching someone to lead better is not so much about transmitting content as it is about transmitting mindsets and thinking skills, specifically analysis, problem-solving, and reflective skills. Coaching outcomes look more like this:

- The coachee will be able to identify where they can grow.
- The coachee will be able to identify where the leadership strengths are.
- The coachee will be able to plan, prepare, and execute solutions for the instructional problems in their school or district.

In sum, a coach's goal is to help their coachee figure out *for themselves* how to do better. That's what creates lasting change. Not telling. Not advising. Those don't always get the buy-in to sink in more than skin deep. Therefore, as leadership coaches, we want the coachees to do most of the talking and doing. We want them to feel like leaders, not students or players or subordinate employees, and that means making the space for them to step into their authority and lead.

It also means that, even when a coachee is wrong, you can't always say they're wrong.

Steve, a charter school principal, said he was a data guru. He claimed charter schools had more flexibility than public schools, which Lorna was willing to concede, and boasted about all the data he used to form his instructional decisions.

"So then, on October first, you'll get the snapshot of all your students, which will count toward your school's accountability. If you know those numbers ahead of time, you can plan your interventions for this semester," Lorna said.

"No, I've never heard of those groups counting for more," Steve said, dismissing Lorna's words, along with this vital piece of data.

Lorna knew identified groups of students counted more toward accountability than unidentified students, but she couldn't force that information onto Steve if she wanted to keep building trust. Steve had a prior coach who had tried to tell Steve what to do instead of allowing him to figure it out on his own, and that approach had failed to make a positive shift. So she would approach him as a partner, not his boss. "Well, my experience is in Texas, but let's look at that data and talk to some people at the state level. There may be information we're missing."

Two sessions and some specialists' information later, Steve's tune changed. "Wow," he said, "there's a lot about data I don't know!" Now Steve knew what he didn't know, and he was more ready to be coached.

Lorna held back her "I told you so." It would be satisfying, but it wouldn't help Steve move forward. So instead she said, "I'm learning a lot about Florida too. Now that we know, what are our next steps?"

As a coach, you aren't just imparting knowledge. You don't lecture your coachee. You facilitate the coachee identifying and solving their own problems. Through conversation and questions, you provide ways the coachee can reflect and assess their progress.

Let's go back to Carmen, Caleb, and Martin again. What other mistake did they make in their coaching approaches? They were not tailoring their sessions to the individual coachee, taking that coachee's Why, BVBs, and goals into account. Everything was the same. Which brings us to the next component of preparing to coach: how to establish an individualized relationship with each coachee.

ESTABLISHING A COACHING RELATIONSHIP

As a teacher, whenever Melinda got called over the intercom to the principal's office at the end of the day, a flood of angst washed over her. She feared she'd done something wrong, even though she couldn't think of what. Nine times out of ten, she wasn't in trouble. In fact, it was a good thing, a request to take on a new project or more responsibilities. But in Melinda's mind, every time was trouble.

When Melinda moved up to principal, then to assistant superintendent, and she got calls from her district supervisors, she still couldn't shake the "I'm in trouble now" feeling. Her personal life is not exempt from this feeling either. When Melinda gets a call from the assisted living facility in which her dad lives, the feeling is there again. "The principal's office called," the family member first to listen to the message says. "Who's going to call back to see what kind of trouble Dad got into today?"

When anyone gets called down to the office by a supervisor, often the immediate reaction is "Oh no, what did I do wrong?" Anxiety rises, creating a situation where people expect consequences and feel the need to hide their vulnerabilities and mistakes to protect their status.

But coaching relies on honesty and vulnerability to work, and you can't give effective feedback to your coachee, or get effective information and feedback from your coachee, if they don't trust you. Trust in your coaching relationship means your coachee wants to work with you and is willing to expose their perceived vulnerabilities (a.k.a. the things they most need to work on). So the first thing a coach has to do is replace the anxiety and resistance someone might feel, or is ready to feel, when meeting a new person by building a relationship. This relationship does not have to be as intimate as that of a friend or therapist—in fact, it's better if it isn't—but you do have to have a collegial relationship built on trust, mutual respect, and curiosity. A partnership and collaboration rather than a top-down, punitive dynamic.

To start establishing this relationship, we share a bit about ourselves at the beginning of every new coaching opportunity and workshop. We do a brief rundown of what got us into education and continue to share snippets of our experiences as educators to illustrate points and to provide demonstrations of how we worked through obstacles similar to the ones facing the coachees. Since trust is built over time, these snippets and stories do not have to be long, and shouldn't be. One dropped in where it can do the most good as a model or demonstration works best.

Coachees don't want to hear all your stories. And you don't need to tell them. Whoever is getting coached needs to do the majority of the talking; that's your goal as a coach. But a few strategic shares like we've talked about before—your Why, your basic BVBs, an illustrative example—expressed in a few sentences can go a long way toward establishing trust. If you expect your coachee to spill their guts, they'll want at least a gesture of that from you to show you're also willing to be vulnerable in front of them.

Our stories change depending on whom we coach. What is shared should align with the topics and experiences the coachee is most interested in. They should serve the coachee, not the coach. The coachee should be able to recognize and relate to what is shared. Since we work with a lot of low-performing, high-poverty, high-minority schools, we relate stories and examples from when we taught or led similar schools.

To succeed, coaches must first work toward building relationships with the coachee so they can trust that they will not be attacked or penalized for revealing what they don't like about their leadership and for working toward getting better at those things, even if there are bumps along the way. Opening up requires trust. Being vulnerable requires trust. Then the growth can happen.

To be a good coach, we have to first change our mindset from that of evaluator, advisor, or teacher to a coaching mindset. We have to move from places of motivating through punishment or taking away points to a place of motivating through encouragement and adding points. The coachee has to want to change and then has to see how that change makes reaching their goals simpler once everything is said and done.

So how do we create a coaching mindset?

THE COACHING MINDSET

We've coached over five hundred educators and administrators as of the writing of this book, and there are always a few in the room who are just there to fill time. In some instances, we are asked to coach leaders who are not meeting the expectations of their supervisors. Often these coaching situations do not work because in a forced relationship, people put up defensive walls before the first meeting even begins. As coaches, it's our job to help the coachee reframe this dynamic, but sometimes, despite our best efforts, that shift doesn't happen. The coachee does not want any part of the experience.

There is no way to build a trusting, open, listening relationship with a person who refuses to let you in. They've been told they need a coach and resist that directive. It makes them the hardest people to coach. Someone coming into a room resistant does not share, does not reflect, does not want to change or acknowledge they need to. They are nowhere near Maxwell's first level of leadership. Therefore, they are not coachable, and they cannot coach others.

One way of changing this attitude, as a coach, is to take up a coaching mindset, an approach much different than a resistant coachee might be used to.

The coaching mindset allows you to put your own agenda aside and allow others to take the lead. It makes you prioritize open-ended questions and encouragement in conversations, instilling a mindset of curiosity, collaboration, and coevolution rather than a mindset of telling and prescribing a single "right" way to do things. It doesn't seek to manage people and knock down their ideas; it seeks to help them manage themselves and the people they are responsible for so they can learn to become better leaders. It opens the floor to new ideas and perspectives, and desires to listen to understand.

As a coach, you aren't a permanent fixture in a school or district, and the goal is to get the coachee to a state of independence where they feel confident in assessing a situation and making effective decisions on their own as they travel through the levels of leadership and change management steps to fix the next problem. To reuse the adage from above, you're teaching them to fish, which always requires losing a few hooks. The key is to not let one lost hook sink your whole fishing trip.

A big part of the coaching mindset will be familiar to educators, as it embraces Carol Dweck's idea of "growth mindset," or the ability to see a skill not as something inherent but as something that needs practice to build.[24] Dweck compares a growth mindset to a fixed mindset, in which people think you're either born with a certain ability or intelligence or you're not, and therefore you can't change what you're good or bad at. But people with growth mindsets believe they can increase areas of skill or intelligence through work and learning. There is no failure or "I'm bad at math"; it's "not *yet*." "I'm not good at math *yet*, but someday, with practice, I can be." This "not yet" mindset means the person must be open to reflect upon their weaknesses and mistakes, learn from them, accept constructive feedback, and try again. It's what we'd also call being "open-minded."

An open-minded leader is someone who's not only willing to listen attentively but is also actively seeking out learning opportunities. They recognize the feeling of imposter syndrome, wherein they know they have the credentials but don't know how to apply and perform in certain situations with those credentials. They may be really good at creating master schedules but may not be so good at giving feedback on classroom instruction.

Openness, here, means openness to change: "Here are my gaps in skill and knowledge. What can I do to fill them?" When someone comes up with a new idea or alternative perspective to fill those gaps, coachable people are open to trying them out and absorbing them into their context. Someone else's solution might be the better way.

Then again, as a coach with more lived experience, you might disagree with the solutions your coachee comes up with, but that doesn't mean you voice that rejection out loud

---

24 Carol S. Dweck, *Mindset: The New Psychology of Success* (Random House, 2006).

or immediately. That solution is rooted in their perspective and Why. But we do have to figure out how to move forward from there. How can you help them see the potential pros and cons of that solution?

Helping your coachee adopt a growth mindset encourages the coachee to focus on development, learning, and continuous improvement. The coach encourages leaders to take ownership over their goals and progress and reflect on mistakes. Learning how failure happens helps prevent those same mistakes in the future and promotes adaptability and confidence that things can truly change as long as the right solution is found.

It is even more important that the coach possesses a growth mindset about the people they help.

> **THE COACH HAS TO BELIEVE THAT THE COACHEE'S ABILITIES AND LEADERSHIP SKILLS CAN BE DEVELOPED, STRATEGIES CAN BE IMPARTED, AND CHALLENGES CAN BE LEARNED FROM.**

In a coaching session, Melinda and her coachee explored various teaching techniques to support EL learners. For example, they discussed using peer modeling to reinforce academic language, but the principal dismissed the idea, arguing that these students wouldn't be able to keep up with their peers regardless of the support provided.

Laura said, "I hear what you're saying, but my school has a high number of special education and EL students. I'm not sure the solutions you suggest are possible here." This told Melinda more about the leader's bias than it did about the students. There was a story in Laura's head blocking her from moving forward. How could Melinda create the trust that would allow her to challenge this leader on her assumptions?

First, she had to listen to understand, not respond. She had to be present in the moment and not think about the repercussions of Laura's beliefs. Listening isn't done to just wait for an opening to respond; it's done to understand the coachee's perspective. To coach well, listen to repeat and validate what the other person is saying and feeling within the context of their own experience before going into helpful mode.

Melinda responded. "So what you're saying is that special education and EL students aren't as capable of achievement. This activity isn't possible for them to do," she repeated back to Laura.

"Um."

Open-ended questions without a yes/no answer, or ones Melinda didn't already know the answer to, would provoke Laura to think. Gentle pressure, as we call this type of questioning, was the recipe here: a balance of support and accountability that keeps leaders moving toward their goals without feeling overwhelmed. It's about maintaining a steady, persistent focus on improvement while providing encouragement, guidance, and space for growth.

"Do you think everyone can succeed and go to college?" Melinda probed.

"Yes," Laura affirmed quickly.

"What's your school's mission for your students?"

She was ready for this one. "That every child will be prepared to go to college or enter the workforce when they graduate."

"So do your beliefs about EL students and their learning capabilities align to your mission and values?"

"Uh, no," Laura admitted.

"What about your behaviors and actions at school? Do they support this mission?"

More thought. "Not totally. Not for all groups of students."

"So how can we adjust your actions so they align with your mission that all students can learn?"

Rapport and trust allowed Laura to accept Melinda's probing questions even when they made her uncomfortable. That was from the relationship they had built in previous sessions.

It's not about being right and wrong; it's about seeing where the coachee is, where they want to go, and how they will get there.

COACHING IS NOT ABOUT TELLING PEOPLE WHAT THEY ARE DOING WRONG; IT'S ABOUT HELPING THEM DO THINGS BETTER.

Not punitive but supportive. We don't write people up; we write things down.

Do you believe the person you are coaching can grow and improve? Are you coaching them to grow or go? Firing should be the last resort of any supervisor. We don't want to go in with a deficit mindset that only sees someone's weaknesses and biases us toward looking for more. We want to go in with a growth mindset that looks for strengths and builds upon those.

The coaching mindset is more reflective than punitive when it comes to finding fault. "What can *I* do better to help this person do better?" Not "What can *they* do better?" Failure isn't blamed on others, but is taken up by the leader.

There are times, we will admit, when a solution *is* wrong, and as an experienced leader and coach, you know it. But sometimes it's just where the coachee is on their journey. They don't know what they don't know. As a coach, the goal is to provide an opportunity for the coachee to not only see things differently and come up with novel solutions, but then to act on those solutions. That takes trust.

The coaching mindset embraces a growth mindset, about both yourself and others. It embraces reflection and feedback to enhance self-awareness of both weaknesses and strengths, be open to new ideas, and most importantly, be open to *trying out* those new ideas and acting upon them. And it acknowledges that this mindset is necessary for both the coach and the coachee to adopt if any positive growth is going to occur.

It's hard to coach someone with a fixed mindset, who thinks they know it all already or can't learn it, because they are closed to growth. They are stuck. They can't get past the barriers of their projected strength or weakness to be vulnerable in their not knowing. Their resistance makes it harder to focus on improving performance and talent, which means they don't grow. And when someone can't grow anymore, they often go, either by their own choice or by force.

We fully acknowledge the coaching mindset is not easy to adopt because it makes us vulnerable, and for some, vulnerability equals weakness. The fear is that revealing we know less than we "should" know means others will take advantage of us. We'll be attacked. We'll be passed over for promotion or pay raises. We'll be fired. We'll lose.

We may say in schools that it's how you run the race, not how you finish. But do we really believe that? Federal and state accountability have set up an environment of competitiveness that's just as rampant as any Texas football field. You have to have the best test scores, the most qualified teachers, the nicest buildings, the highest rating. As a principal or district leader, you're expected to come in with skills and knowledge that our learn-as-you-go promotional system did not give you to start.

Competitiveness focused on a final "win" does not lead people to prioritize the process of getting better together. It does not encourage us to collaborate or help each other get across the finish line. Instead, we protect ourselves by hiding our weaknesses and the things that do not serve us or others. In this way, educators are not exempt from the fears of our students, who may prefer to not speak at all rather than offer an answer that may be wrong.

We, as educators, tell students every day that it's okay to make mistakes, to not know what they don't know. We meet them where they are. But when do we, as leaders, give ourselves that same grace and space? When do we allow ourselves to grow?

What if vulnerability does not equate to weakness? What if to be vulnerable is to be willing to admit there are things you don't know? As consultants and coaches, we certainly admit we don't know everything, which makes us open to learning.

As educators, we value lifelong learning and understand the vast depth of human wisdom. Modeling the vulnerable mindset of "not yet" should be seen as a strength in our profession.

BECOMING A LEADER SHOULD NOT MEAN LOSING THE TEACHER WITHIN US.

Failures and setbacks will happen, and when we accept this fact, we can turn those mistakes into opportunities for learning and growth.

The coaching relationship cannot survive based on "Gotcha!" moments. As coaches, we aren't out to find people doing wrong; we are out to find people doing right and help them build off that rightness. We are also there to hear confessions of mistakes and weak skillsets so we can discover the opportunities for growth. Since coaching is all about getting better to lead better, we have to discover the areas that *can* get better and have the most area for improvement. It's like filling potholes in a road. But we can only help someone fill their potholes for a smoother ride if they show them to us.

You can't be coached if you are afraid. No lasting change, no growth, comes from forced change. But we can take out that fear factor if systems are put in place that prioritize collaborative leadership building and a more positive leadership stance.

CONCLUSION

Coaching at its best is a partnership, one grounded in trust, reflection, and a shared commitment to growth. While the primary aim is to support the coachee in achieving their goals and outcomes, the most powerful coaching relationships are reciprocal. The coach enters the space not as an expert with all the answers, but as a partner in learning, open to being shaped by the process, the people, and the purpose of the work.

Coachees who are truly ready to be coached don't come with a know-it-all mindset. They arrive with curiosity, humility, and the belief that even as leaders, they are still learners.

They acknowledge that stepping into new roles or challenges means there is always more to discover, refine, and improve. This is the essence of a growth mindset, a belief that abilities and intelligence can be developed through effort, feedback, and perseverance.

When both coach and coachee bring this mindset to the table, coaching becomes more than a strategy; it becomes a powerful catalyst for transformation. It's in this space of mutual respect and learning that sustainable leadership growth begins. This is when you know you're not just coaching; you're leading with purpose, modeling the very mindset you hope to inspire in others.

WORK SESSION 5: PRACTICING A COACHING MINDSET

Principal Kiki sat quietly after the staff meeting, replaying one teacher's frustrated comment in her mind: *"We've tried everything with these students, and nothing works."* The words stung, not because she doubted the staff's effort, but because they revealed something deeper: a sense of helplessness, maybe even resignation.

Later that afternoon, during a coaching call, Kiki brought it up. "I think we've hit a wall," she admitted. "Some of my team seems to believe that certain students just can't improve. And honestly, after the year we've had, I'm starting to feel it too." Her coach paused and then asked, "How do we shift from a fixed mindset to a growth one, individually and as a school?"

That question stayed with Kiki long after the call ended. She reflected on how she often talked about data and achievement, but rarely about learning from failure or celebrating progress. She realized that a growth mindset wasn't just a poster in a classroom; it had to be a leadership stance.

Over the next week, Kiki started small. She began her next staff meeting with a story of a student who'd made a huge leap academically, not because of a new program, but because a teacher believed in his potential and adjusted her approach. She invited teachers to reflect on their own assumptions about who could succeed. And most importantly, she began modeling vulnerability herself, sharing moments when she didn't get it right the first time and what she learned from them.

Kiki knew change wouldn't happen overnight. But for the first time in a while, she felt energized. She wasn't just trying to improve test scores; she was trying to build a culture where adults and students alike believed they could grow.

Key Actions and Reflections

School Leader Thought Work

- Where do you see fixed mindset beliefs showing up among your team or even in yourself?
- How do you talk about failure and learning in your school? Is it seen as part of the process or something to avoid?
- What are small but visible ways you can begin modeling and promoting a growth mindset culture?

District Leader Thought Work

- How are growth mindset principles embedded into your leadership development efforts?
- In what ways do district structures and policies support or hinder schools in taking learning risks and growing from setbacks?
- How could you support principals like Kiki in shifting their school culture toward one of learning, persistence, and continuous improvement?

PART 3

SIMPLE Coaching

CHAPTER 6

Coaching Approaches

"Coaches have to watch for what they don't want to see and listen for what they don't want to hear."
—John Madden, NFL football coach

Melinda's going to admit something vulnerable here: to start, her early days as a coach were filled with trial, error, and valuable lessons that shaped her practice. Melinda started executive coaching in 2016 full time. She coached fifteen people. That was her job for the next two years. She had a ton of experience as a leader at the classroom, campus, and district level. She felt confident going in to coach her group of new assistant principals and principals.

At the end of her first year of coaching, Melinda thought she'd done a good job. However, she couldn't quite shake the angst of her performance: had she done a good job? Her end-of-the-year evaluation came in from all her coachees, and…they tore her apart.

"She always pulls up the action plan without asking me about my work and what I'm doing."

"She wants to focus on getting things done rather than listening to me."

"I don't think she sees me at all."

Melinda called Lorna—who was already a certified coach, having completed all of her iPEC training—distraught. "I'm not cut out for this. No matter what I try, I don't feel effective!"

"You're not a bad coach, Melinda; you'd just be more impactful with other strategies," Lorna soothed.

Melinda paused. She was too smart to have any of this placating nonsense.

"Well, what did they tell you?" Lorna asked mildly.

"They felt like I didn't build a relationship with them! That I went in to do a job. They never felt like I connected with them," Melinda admitted, reluctantly sharing her failure.

Melinda could feel Lorna's nod at the other end of the phone. "That feedback is hard to take."

But that was the thing. Melinda *did* know what she was doing: what she always did and what she was good at. Her personal leadership style was very task and outcome oriented. If she was told to do something, then darn it, she was going to do it. So when she received the leadership action plan from her supervisors and was told to follow it, that's what she did. She went into her sessions with her coachees and did that plan, checked off all the boxes. Obviously, that approach had not worked with her coachees.

Melinda needed to do something different if she wanted to continue with her coaching job. She met with Lorna on a regular basis to get coached on how to coach, going over scenarios and role-playing what to say. Lorna would give her feedback: what she'd done well, what hadn't gone so well, and why. And Lorna was generous with the tools she'd used successfully, tools Melinda would take and make her own.

Melinda would get her certification in coaching the next year, which gave her the tools and self-assessments that allowed her to recognize her strengths and weaknesses and get better as a coach. There would be no more "she's only here for the job" comments!

Melinda would shift her focus from getting the tasks checked off, even if she was doing the work herself, to putting the ownership and opportunity to complete the tasks on her coachees. She realized all her forms and templates were only tools to get to the goal, not the goal itself. Melinda learned to personalize her new bank of tools and resources so they'd work for the coachee. Instead of directive coaching, like a supervisor would do, as she'd done before, she was practicing collaborative coaching, the technique used by leadership coaches.

Our hope is that emerging coaches can use the coaching theories, strategies, and tools we've gathered through our years of coaching experience to help them be better coaches too. No one should have to reinvent the wheel when it's already being used elsewhere. Work smarter, not harder, yes?

As you can see from the story above, Melinda didn't start out feeling confident or fully prepared to coach. She didn't know exactly where she stood, and maybe you don't either. But what made the difference wasn't having it all figured out. It was the willingness to grow.

> **COACHING ISN'T ABOUT BEING PERFECT; IT'S ABOUT SHOWING UP WITH HUMILITY, LEARNING ALONG THE WAY, AND STAYING COMMITTED TO THE PEOPLE YOU SUPPORT.**

It's time to start creating your own system for coaching others.

IDENTIFYING LEADERSHIP STRENGTHS

One of the key focuses of our coaching is helping coachees identify their skill and character strengths—and understand how to carry those strengths into their new leadership role without feeling like imposters. They may be novices in certain aspects, yes, but not imposters. While there are always new leadership and job-specific skills to learn, coachees arrive with the strengths that made them successful in previous roles. By recognizing and leveraging these core strengths, they can build a confidence-boosting foundation for growth in their current position and pursue their future passions and goals with clarity and purpose.

This is the part of coaching that's always fun! Coaching is primarily about nurturing and expanding what the coachee is already good at, while also focusing on improving areas that need development. Play to your strengths, right? You don't have to be a math whiz to observe good math classroom instruction; you just need to know what the tenets of good instruction are. Coaching can help you identify those big-picture criteria.

Use strengths to help grow and facilitate areas of improvement.

> **BUILD THE WEAKER LEADERSHIP MUSCLES SO YOU CAN BECOME A WHOLE LEADER.**

Identifying leadership strengths and areas of improvement further enhances leadership coaching. You both learn about your own strengths before the session and know the strengths of your coachee, strengths you can encourage the coachee to grow in order to become a stronger leader in this area.

For instance, Melinda's strengths consistently show a commitment to student learning and holding people accountable for performance. She leads with a system to support these outcomes. She likes using data systems to help her coachees grow or to look at her business processes and structures to ensure they support her commitment to her coachees and staff. Melinda's coachees need to know student learning and holding people accountable for performance are two of Melinda's strengths and big internal motivators. Results-driven strength. If you coach her, ask "What results do you want to see?" She likes to see projects come to fruition.

One of Lorna's strengths is strategy. Lorna likes to see how all the pieces work together. "What's the connection between A and B, and how does that impact C?" She wants to see the full picture and then drill down from there, versus starting with small details and moving toward larger systems. Lorna also needs to process. We can hash out ideas for an hour, but we won't be able to make any decision on those ideas or take action until Lorna's slept on it. When Lorna writes an email, she does not send it right away. She knows she'll have different ideas in an hour that will cause her to rewrite it three times until she gets to where she wants to be. A coach would need to know Lorna's not comfortable acting right away and will need to come back to any new proposals at the next session. She doesn't just take action when given a task; she needs to think it through first.

Once both coach and coachee knows their strengths, it'll be easier to select a coaching approach that works for both.

SELECTING A COACHING APPROACH

There are many types of "coaches," and we thought it useful at this time to go through what and who they are. We, of course, have our own bias for what kind of coaching works best to get results. We bet you can guess which one.

COACH VERSUS MENTOR

Many people use the terms *mentor* and *coach* interchangeably, but these are two different approaches to leadership development.

A coach, often formally assigned to a coachee, guides the conversation by asking open-ended questions that encourage the coachee to reflect, explore, and find solutions. The aim is to help the coachee achieve a specific goal or overcome a challenge, but the direction of the goal is set by the coachee themselves. While the coach leads the process, the coachee takes the lead in identifying the problem and defining the desired outcome. The coaching process is structured with a general framework, outlining how the conversation unfolds from start to finish but always driven by the coachee's objectives and growth.

The coach doesn't necessarily have experience in the same role as the coachee, or even the same industry. It helps to have a common background when the coach may want to slip into the mentor role and say, "Have you tried this tool? It worked well for me in a similar situation," but it isn't necessary. This very open-ended, "let's figure it out together" form of true leadership coaching sounds very different from the athletic coaching people in education may be more familiar with. A football coach isn't going to let the players figure out how to develop or make the rules of the game for themselves.

A mentor is someone who has served in a similar role to the one their mentee now occupies. The mentee is typically less experienced and may not have all the resources or tools they need to perform their role effectively. The mentor offers periodic advice and shares tools that worked well for them in a more informal manner. Mentoring relationships tend to be flexible, with conversations happening as needed, and don't always follow a structured format or timeline. These relationships are often chosen by both the mentor and mentee rather than being assigned.

When coaching a school or district leader, knowing when to coach versus when to mentor often comes down to understanding the coachee's needs in the moment and the level of guidance they require. Use coaching when the leader benefits from self-discovery and developing their problem-solving skills; this approach is valuable when they have the foundation to analyze issues independently but need support in refining their strategies or exploring new perspectives. Coaching is ideal when the goal is to build confidence in their ability to navigate challenges on their own.

On the other hand, mentoring is more suitable when the leader needs guidance, such as insights from your personal experience, advice on navigating complex situations, or specific recommendations for best practices. Mentoring can be particularly helpful when the coachee faces unfamiliar challenges or transitions and needs a more directive approach to gain clarity.

At times, you need to step into the role of a mentor, and

at other times, you need to adopt the approach of a coach. Balancing these two approaches allows you, as the coach, to be responsive to the coachee's development, moving between coaching and mentoring as the coachee grows in skill and confidence.

EVALUATOR/SUPERVISOR

Some districts we've approached tell us they don't need coaches because the school or district supervisors are coaches. A supervisor is a boss, to put it simply. They evaluate faculty and staff performance and, as such, have power over hiring, promotion, reprimand, and termination. This power to decide the fate of others automatically sets up a power imbalance that leads to mistrust and anxiety. When are these leaders coaches, and when are they bosses? The distinction can be murky, and people sometimes aren't willing to share their weaknesses and challenges with someone who has the power to promote or demote them.

Research indicates that power dynamics significantly influence the effectiveness of coaching relationships.[25] When a coach holds significantly more power than the coachee, it can hinder open communication and trust, essential components of a successful coaching partnership. Conversely, when the relationship is more egalitarian, with mutual respect and balanced power, it fosters a more productive and supportive environment. Therefore, maintaining a coaching relationship characterized by equality is crucial for its success.

---

25 Carmen Knudson-Martin, "Why Power Matters: Creating a Foundation of Mutual Support in Couple Relationships," *Family Process* 52, no. 1 (2013): 5–18, https://doi.org/10.1111/famp.12011.

Confidentiality also becomes a problem when a supervisor is filling dual roles. A coaching relationship is confidential. Nothing revealed in those conversations, except something expressly illegal, will be told to anyone outside that coaching session. It will not go on their permanent evaluations or end up in their file. Mistakes will not follow them around. At the most, we'll transparently tell our coachees that broad themes will be reported to their district leadership in order to better plan future professional development and create systems of support. If a coachee acknowledges a mistake, that should not be held against them in a promotion interview. However, even the most ethical supervisors may find it challenging to overlook past mistakes and shortcomings when they're involved in making decisions about promotions or future employment opportunities, especially when considering someone for advancement based on their performance.

Therefore, we caution against supervisors being coaches to those they supervise.

DIRECTIVE COACHING

Directive coaching, simply put, is telling someone what to do. It sets up a managerial, top-down relationship: "This is what you need to do, and this is how you should do it." It may be no surprise here that directive coaching is the style we most often find when supervisors are also coaches.

Even if the directive is the right thing to do, as we've already pointed out, the change may not be successfully adopted and sustained because the coachee has no personal investment in the idea. It isn't theirs. They don't understand the reasons or the process behind what they are doing. They don't understand how results are tied to actions. They go through the motions, and the lack of investment and understanding shows. "I did exactly what she told me to do, and it didn't work" is often the result.

Directive coaching can come off as pedantic and condescending if done poorly, like the coachee isn't smart enough to figure out what's best for them. However, when applied appropriately, directive coaching can be highly effective in providing clear guidance and structure, especially when a coachee is new to a role or facing a complex challenge. The key is to balance direction with respect, ensuring that the coachee feels empowered to take ownership of their growth while benefiting from the coach's expertise.

INSTRUCTIONAL COACHING

Instructional coaching is an interaction between a coach and coachee based on the coachee's needs. Often, the instructional coach provides a menu of processes and skills that will help solve a coachee's problem. The coachee can select from this menu and adapt their selection to their situation, so there's a little knowledge sharing, a little mentoring and advice thrown in. Questions you might hear in an instructional coaching session include "If you tried X, what do you think would happen? What do you need to adapt in this scenario for this strategy to work for you and your school?" The coachee might share a process for analyzing data or share thinking about a solution. The coach shares strategies they've used that worked well, then the coachee and coach think together on which strategy may work best, then the coachee executes the strategy on their own. If you think this type of coaching feels akin to a facilitative teacher-student relationship, you'd be right. Here are the tools; here's how I built my house with them; now how are you going to build your house?

The normal process is a round of planning with the coachee, plus the coachee's suggested solution and rationale behind that solution. This is a facilitative and collaborative type of coaching, where both coachee and coach are on equal footing and coachee leads the conversation. These are the types of coaches perhaps most commonly found in schools.

Instructional coaching offers significant benefits when applied to school and district leaders. By working closely with leaders, a coach helps them refine their leadership practices, focusing on areas such as goal setting, decision-making, and fostering a positive school culture. Through personalized, reflective conversations, the coach supports the leader in identifying specific challenges, setting clear objectives, and implementing strategies tailored to their unique context. This collaborative partnership builds the leader's confidence, strengthens their skillset, and enhances their ability to guide their teams, ultimately leading to improved outcomes for both teachers and students.

COLLABORATIVE COACHING

Collaborative coaching is rooted in shared problem-solving, where the coachee drives the thinking and decision-making. Rather than offering solutions, the coach uses open-ended questions to guide reflection and support the coachee in identifying their own strategies.

The process begins by the coach and the coachee defining a problem of practice and envisioning success together. From there, coach and coachee brainstorm together, but the coachee leads the way. Suggestions from the coach are offered as possibilities, not prescriptions, reinforcing the coachee's ownership of the work.

When Melinda and Lorna coach collaboratively, even during data analysis, they avoid pointing out problems. Instead, they explore the data with leaders, prompting insight and shared discovery.

Collaborative coaching takes time, but it builds deeper learning and sustainable change. It's not about quick fixes; it's about growing leaders who can solve problems long after the coach is gone.

FACILITATIVE COACHING

A good leadership coach, whether in business or in education, facilitates the coachee in figuring out what they need to know, what they need to solve, and how they need to solve it. A space is created to think through a new role and the decisions that go along with it, without fear of punitive evaluations or ostracization for asking for help.

Facilitative coaching only happens when you coach a leader who has a growth mindset and is open to coaching. They want to be a better person to be a better leader. They are ready, willing, and able—or, as we like to say, they have the skill and the will to get there.

When combined, collaborative and facilitative coaching creates a dynamic, flexible approach that empowers the coachee while providing the structure and support they need to succeed. In this integrated model, the coach and coachee engage in a shared partnership where the coach facilitates reflection, asks thought-provoking questions, and helps guide the coachee through a structured process. At the same time, the coach ensures that the coachee takes an active role in identifying challenges, setting goals, and developing solutions. This hybrid approach blends the strength of collaboration—fostering mutual problem-solving—with the power of facilitation, which encourages independent thinking and personal ownership of the growth process.

CONCLUSION

The best coaching approaches empower leaders to take ownership of their own growth and goals. So to break it down:

- Instructional—Let's come up with those ideas together.
- Collaborative—We're going to come up with ideas together.
- Facilitative—I'm going to empower you to make your own decisions based on the impact and outcomes you think will result.

Find your strengths as a coach. Find your approach. There are many ways to coach and be a coach, but the best, most effective ways that give the most bang for the buck are neutral and collaborative at their core.

TOOL: SELF REFLECTION FOR CHOOSING YOUR COACHING APPROACH

Use this tool to guide your decision-making and strengthen the intentionality of your coaching conversations. Great coaching happens in the moment but is grounded in thoughtful design.

Purpose: Use this tool to intentionally apply the coaching approach—Instructional, Collaborative, or Facilitative—that best meets the needs of your coachee and the moment.

Overview of Coaching Approaches

APPROACH	WHEN TO USE IT	WHAT IT LOOKS LIKE	SAMPLE COACHING MOVES
Instructional	When the coachee needs specific expertise, direction, or support to build a new skill	You provide guidance, model strategies, or give direct feedback.	—"Let me model what that looks like." "Here's one area to target based on the data."
Collaborative	When you and the coachee share ownership in analyzing data, planning, or problem-solving	You partner as equals, co-constructing solutions and strategies.	—"Let's brainstorm some strategies together." "What do you notice about the results?"
Facilitative	When the goal is to build reflection, self-awareness, and leadership ownership	You ask reflective questions that draw out insight and build internal capacity.	—"What values are guiding your decisions?" "What might be getting in the way?"

Coaching Moves in Action: Effective coaches flow between these approaches during a single session based on the coachee's skill/will and the challenge at hand.

Before your next coaching session, ask:

- What is the goal of this conversation?
- What does the coachee need most right now?
- Which approach—or blend—will best support their growth?

CHAPTER 7

Skill and Will

"The will must be stronger than the skill."
—MUHAMMAD ALI, PROFESSIONAL
BOXER AND SOCIAL ACTIVIST

We were working with a school, and part of our design plan was to go in and help them think through the current systems they had in place and new systems they wanted to create. We sat down with Principal Anand, looking at his data that supported that the school had been in a state of help, or comprehensive school improvement (CSI) status, for more than five years. Something in the current approach wasn't producing the desired results, so we were partnering with Principal Anand to explore new strategies and support meaningful change.

Lorna asked Principal Anand, "What do you think you need to help your students become more engaged in the school learning environment and increase attendance?"

Adamantly, he said, "Project-based learning. That's the answer."

They knew from experience in instruction that project-based learning for a CSI school was not the answer. Not yet, anyway.

Melinda and Lorna decided to not do their usual follow-up of "Tell me how you think project-based learning is going to be the answer." This would take a more direct approach.

"I'm not sure that's the direction you need to go in," Melinda stated. "In our experience, project-based learning is something to put in place in a school that's already doing well academically and you want to increase the options for learning modalities."

Principal Anand's face shuddered. "I don't think that's right. I think this is what we need to do to fix our school."

Sometimes as a coach you can't help but interject your own strong beliefs into the conversation, and it shuts down the coachee. How do you circle back around to rebuild the relationship you just damaged? How do you reframe?

"Okay," Melinda said, knowing anything more in disagreement would harden the principal more toward her suggestions.

He pressed them: "If it comes to the point where we can't agree, then we're just at an impasse and I'm going to have to end our coaching relationship."

"That's fine," Lorna agreed, not taking his bait. "We'll sit on that until that time comes." If she didn't give him anything to fight against, he'd be forced to fight with himself.

Coaches don't engage in battles of will.

A COACH DOESN'T "WIN" BY BEING RIGHT OR HAVING THE COACHEE FOLLOW THEIR WILL.

That's exactly the opposite of what a coach wants. The principal didn't know what he didn't know. He was low skill/high will. They'd back off and give him some time to process his decision and to reflect on standards-based instruction.

The next day, Principal Andad had a change of heart. "Yeah, you might be right," he conceded. "Project-based learning probably isn't the way to go. Maybe we do need to focus on grade-level standards before we focus on project-based learning."

A lot of the coachees who get stuck when being coached fall into a level of both skill and will. We've come across leaders who fall into all four skill/will quadrants, and part of the job of a coach is being able to pinpoint where a coachee sits at any given moment so the coaching approach can alter accordingly and keep everything moving, kind of like adjusting the GPS before they take a wrong turn and end up in a drive-through when they were aiming for the highway.

To explain, *skill* is the ability to do a task.

Will is the drive to do that task. (We're referring to will*ing*ness here, not will*ful*ness.)

Here are the combinations.

LOW SKILL/LOW WILL

The leader has limited knowledge in this area and, as a result, may not yet recognize the need for change. They think they're fine and know enough to get by. They are not interested in growing. They are not interested in change. This can be a coachee who has been in their position for a while and is comfortable with the way things are. Often these coachees are assigned a coach as a last resort before they are let go or moved to a nonleadership position.

This doesn't mean these coachees aren't intelligent; in fact, many are incredibly smart. But they may be low in skill for the role they currently hold and out of their depth, whether they realize it or not. What makes them challenging to coach is that true growth only begins when they're willing to acknowledge what they don't yet know. Once that awareness clicks, their willingness to learn increases, and that's when meaningful coaching can begin.

LOW SKILL/HIGH WILL

The leader has limited knowledge in this area, recognizes the gap, and is eager to grow and improve. This can be a newly transitioned or promoted coachee and is also assigned a coach, but their eagerness to accept feedback and develop new skills can make them a joy to coach and can put the coach more in a mentoring role as the coachee dives in and does most of the work. They may have even chosen to be coached by seeking out a coaching program or coach on their own.

HIGH SKILL/VARIABLE WILL

The leader brings a wealth of skills but believes their current approach is sufficient and shows little interest in further growth or change. This can be a coachee who's been in their position for a while or someone who doesn't want to admit they need help in a new role. They've had a coach assigned to them. These are the most difficult coachees to coach, as they know enough to get by as a leader and want to keep their high-level roles and often don't think they need a coach.

HIGH SKILL/HIGH WILL

The leader possesses a strong skillset and is eager to continue learning. This coachee may have been in their position for some time, is a learner, and is looking to advance to the next role or make significant improvements in their outcomes. Hopefully every coachee gets to this point, as leaders who fall into this context are self-starters and take ownership of their weaknesses and mistakes. When something goes wrong, they ask, "What can I do better next time?"

To coach someone well, it is useful to see where the coachee falls in these categories when first starting out. Sometimes the coachee can progress through these categories, though it isn't necessarily a straight line. For instance, someone who's always had the mindset of a lifelong learner may always have high will, though their skills may be low or high depending on the role they currently hold.

Once you, as the coach, identify where the coachee falls in the Skill/Will Context, you can select the tools you will need to coach them up. This may require strategic use of different coaching types depending on where the coachee is at in their growth.

These skill and will categories can generally be mapped onto Maxwell's 4 Phases of Leadership that appear in an earlier chapter, but these are not always hard-and-fast correlations.

COMBINING MAXWELL'S 4 PHASES OF LEADERSHIP AND THE SKILL/WILL MATRIX

Combining the Skill/Will framework with Maxwell's 4 Phases of Leadership enhances coaching by offering a more holistic approach to leadership development. This synthesis allows coaches to assess a leader's competence and motivation at each stage of their growth, enabling tailored coaching strategies. Whether the focus is on building skills or boosting motivation, coaches can adapt their approach to meet the coachee's specific needs. By aligning both models, coaches can provide targeted support that fosters not only technical proficiency but also the mindset and willpower necessary for sustained leadership growth and success.

PHASE 1: "I DON'T KNOW WHAT I DON'T KNOW"
Skill/Will Quadrant: Low Skill/Low Will
Coaching Strategy

- Focus: Awareness building and basic understanding
- Approach: Provide clear guidance, introduce new concepts, and build confidence. Use direct instruction and mentoring to spark interest and increase motivation.

Coaching Questions: These questions are designed to help the leader gain clarity on identifying areas for growth and build the motivation to engage more deeply in their leadership development.

Awareness Building

- Goal: Encourage reflection on current issues and gaps in knowledge.
    - What do you believe are the most pressing challenges in your school/district?
    - What specific areas of your leadership do you feel need the most improvement?

- What recent successes or challenges have highlighted areas where you feel you could grow as a leader?
- Goal: Clarify their goals and how they align with the school's or district's mission/vision.
  - What specific outcomes are you hoping to achieve that will further the mission/vision of your school or district?
  - What strategies do you use to develop realistic goals with impactful action steps?
  - How do you track the progress of the action steps that contribute to achieving your goals?

Introducing New Concepts

- Goal: Begin introducing foundational leadership concepts.
  - What do you find most challenging in your current role, and why do you think that is?
  - What skills do you think would make the biggest difference in your effectiveness as a leader?
  - How do you envision your role evolving, and what would you like to achieve moving forward?
- Goal: Identify gaps in knowledge and provide an opportunity to introduce new ideas.
  - How do you usually approach challenges at work, and what might help you approach them differently?
  - What's one thing you've been avoiding or reluctant to try in your role? What makes it difficult?
  - If there was a simple step you could take today to feel more equipped, what would that look like?

Building Confidence and Motivation

- Goal: Focus on achievable goals that can build confidence.
  - What is one small, manageable change you could make this week that would make a difference in your leadership?
  - What is something you can commit to right now that feels realistic and will help you progress in your role?
  - If you set one goal for this month, what will that goal look like, and how can you measure your progress?
- Goal: Establish a supportive coaching relationship and build a personalized development plan.
  - What areas of leadership would you like to feel more confident in, and what could we do to address them together?
  - What type of feedback or encouragement would help you stay on track in your development?
  - What would a successful coaching relationship look like to you, and how can we tailor this process to meet your needs?

PHASE 2: "I KNOW WHAT I DON'T KNOW"
Skill/Will Quadrant: Low Skill/High Will
Coaching Strategy

- Focus: Skill development and targeted learning
- Approach: Encourage learning through experience, set achievable goals, and provide constructive feedback. Leverage the individual's high motivation to focus on acquiring the necessary skills.

Coaching Questions: These questions are designed to help the leader focus on targeted skill development, encourage hands-on learning, and set clear, achievable goals that leverage their high motivation.

Skill Development

- Goal: Help the leader identify and prioritize the skills they need to develop and strengthen.
    - What parts of your role feel the most challenging right now?
    - Which tasks or responsibilities take the most time or energy for you to complete?
    - Are there areas where you feel less confident, even though you're eager to improve?
- Goal: Encourage honest self-assessment and create a development plan.
    - What feedback have you received that might help you reflect on your leadership skills?
    - What's one area you feel motivated to improve, even if it feels uncomfortable right now?
    - What would a realistic development plan look like for you over the next sixty to ninety days?
- Goal: Motivate the leader to take initiative and learn by doing.
    - What's one action you could take this week to build confidence in an area you're still learning?
    - What's something you've observed another leader do that you'd like to try for yourself?
    - If you had no fear of making a mistake, what would you experiment with in your role?

Constructive Feedback and Support

- Goal: Reinforce the coaching relationship and ensure the leader feels supported.
    - What's felt most helpful in our work together so far?
    - Where do you feel most supported—and where could you use more guidance?
    - What's helped you stay motivated through the challenges you've faced so far?

PHASE 3: "I GROW AND KNOW AND IT STARTS TO SHOW"
Skill/Will Quadrant: High Skill/Variable Will
Coaching Strategy

- Focus: Refinement and confidence building
- Approach: Support skill application and encourage taking on more complex tasks. If will is low, reconnect with the individual's initial motivations. If will is high, empower them to lead projects or mentor others.

Coaching Questions: These questions are designed to help the leader refine their skills, build confidence, and either reconnect with their motivations or channel their high will into impactful leadership actions.

Skill Refinement

- Goal: Help the leader identify strengths and areas for skill refinement.
    - Which skills do you feel most confident in, and how do you use them to your advantage?
    - How do others typically describe your strengths, and what feedback have you received that you agree with?

- What skills would you like to develop further to help you perform even better in your current role?
- Goal: Encourage reflection on successes and leverage them for continued growth.
  - What tasks or challenges do you find yourself excelling at, and why do you think that is?
  - What recent successes are you most proud of, and what do you think contributed to those outcomes?
  - How can you build on the strategies that worked in your recent successes to achieve even greater results?
  - How did you feel when you achieved those successes, and how can you recreate that feeling in future challenges?

Motivation Alignment (If Will Is Low)

- Goal: Reconnect with the leader's intrinsic motivations.
  - What aspects of your role energize you the most, and how can we ensure you're spending more time on these areas?
  - What personal values or principles drive you in your leadership role, and how can you tap into those values more often?
  - What would it look like if you brought more of your authentic self into your work, and how would that change your approach?
  - How can you create moments in your day or week that remind you of the deeper purpose behind your leadership role?
- Goal: Identify and address factors that may be diminishing motivation.
  - Have you recently encountered any challenges or frus-

trations that have impacted your motivation? How can we address these?
- What part of your leadership role do you find least fulfilling, and why do you think that is?
- Are there external factors (like workload, support, or recognition) that are impacting your motivation, and what changes would help you feel more engaged?
- What do you think has changed in your mindset or perspective that might be affecting your drive to move forward?

PHASE 4: "I SIMPLY GO BECAUSE I KNOW"
Skill/Will Quadrant: High Skill/High Will
Coaching Strategy

- Focus: Autonomy and leadership
- Approach: Delegate responsibility, encourage innovation, and focus on strategic thinking. Provide opportunities for the individual to lead and develop others, ensuring continuous growth and engagement.

Coaching Questions: These questions are designed to help the leader capitalize on their high skill and motivation by focusing on strategic leadership, fostering innovation, effectively delegating, and continuously developing both themselves and others.

Delegation and Developing Others

- Goal: Encourage the development of future leaders by delegating meaningful responsibilities.
    - How do you determine which team members are ready

to take on more responsibility, and how can you start identifying those potential leaders?
- Who on your team do you see as having high potential, and how can you support their growth through delegation?
- What tasks or responsibilities could you delegate to others that would help them grow and prepare for leadership roles?
- What kind of support or feedback can you offer your team members to help them succeed and continue growing as leaders?
- How can you ensure that you're not just delegating tasks, but also fostering the leadership skills and mindset needed for future growth?

Continuous Growth and Engagement
- Goal: Focus on sustaining motivation and engagement.
  - How do you stay motivated and engaged in your role, and how can you maintain this energy over the long term?
  - What challenges do you foresee in the future, and how are you preparing yourself and your team to meet them?
  - How do you keep your team or colleagues engaged and motivated, and what strategies can you adopt to sustain that engagement long term?
  - When you face setbacks, how do you regain your enthusiasm, and what steps can you take to bounce back quickly?
  - What goals or milestones are you most excited about achieving, and how can you break them down to keep momentum going?

Coaching Phases Framework

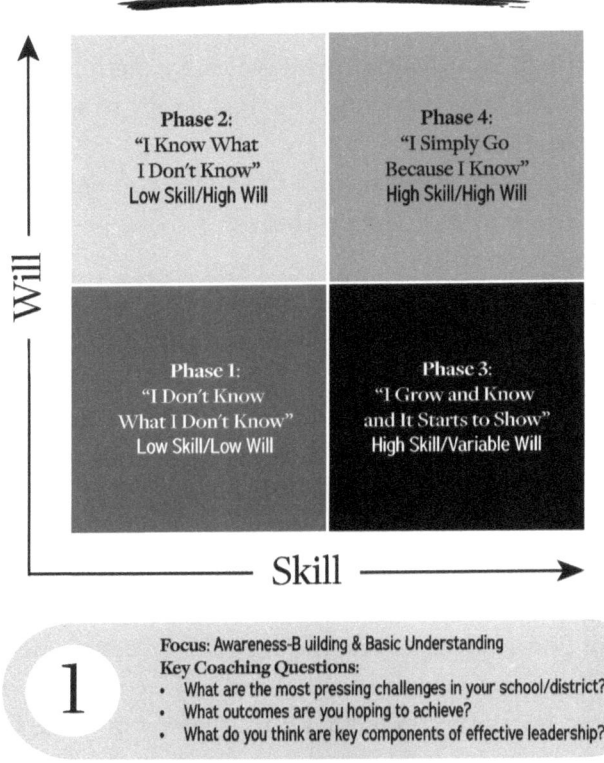

1 — Focus: Awareness-Building & Basic Understanding
Key Coaching Questions:
- What are the most pressing challenges in your school/district?
- What outcomes are you hoping to achieve?
- What do you think are key components of effective leadership?

2 — Focus: Skill Development & Targeted Learning
Key Coaching Questions:
- What specific skills do you need to develop?
- How can you apply what you've learned in real-time situations?
- What short-term goals can you set for skill-building?

3 — Focus: Refinement & Confidence-Building
Key Coaching Questions:
- What recent successes have you experienced?
- What advanced skills would you like to master?
- What helps you feel more confident in your leadership?

4 — Focus: Autonomy & Strategic Leadership
Key Coaching Questions:
- How are you using your autonomy to drive strategic goals?
- What innovative ideas are you considering?
- How can you delegate effectively to develop others?

Skill/Will Context + Phases of Leadership

WHEN COACHING TO GROW TURNS TO COACHING TO GO

As a coach, you need your coachee's willingness to grow before you can help them improve their skills. The coachee must have the willingness to change and do better, for themselves and their school, for coaching to work. If the coachee already comes in with high will, well, don't squander that gift by introducing mistrust that turns high will to low.

We're always of the opinion that we should try every option, coaching to grow instead of coaching to go. We never assume someone is uncoachable, though they may have had failed coaching cycles before. Too often, districts have little patience for development, and one or two missed opportunities means you're on your way out the door. Just as we wouldn't give up on a student who makes a couple mistakes, especially in environments where they're not set up for success, we don't give up on leaders who may be in similar situations. If the coachee has the will to get better, well, we're going to try our darndest to get them better.

But sometimes, as much as we hate it as educators, the coachee refuses to allow anyone to help them to grow. When this happens, there may be only one thing left for the coachee's supervisors to do: let them go. It's a hard fact, but one that must be acknowledged. If a school truly wants to change, the people who serve that school must also want to change. If they can't, or won't, then they are no help to the school's mission and vision and have to part ways with the school.

CONCLUSION

SUCCESSFUL COACHING RELIES ON A COACH'S AWARENESS OF A COACHEE'S SKILL AND WILL, WHICH CORRESPOND TO THEIR LEADERSHIP PHASE.

Understanding these factors helps guide the coaching approach and informs the next strategy in the SIMPLE Coaching Framework to ensure continued success.

CHAPTER 8

The SIMPLE Coaching Framework

"Frameworks are not formulas, they're scaffolds that support deep thinking, shared understanding, and transformational growth."
—Elena Aguilar, author of *The Art of Coaching*

As an elementary school teacher, Melinda had her personal "love units," which are the units every teacher likes to do because they're fun and cute and often connect to a culturally important holiday. In second grade, Melinda taught one of her favorite love units, a collage activity in which students decorated a paper pumpkin with paint, crayon, or pictures from magazines they cut up. It was a reward for her English language arts (ELA) block after a spelling test.

However, Melinda eventually realized the pumpkin collage was nothing more than a time filler. She was teaching a language arts class at a Title I school with only 50 percent proficiency in ELA for second graders. Part of her school's new planning process to close this achievement gap was to review class activities to see if they aligned with the ELA standards. So Melinda had to ask herself, how did pumpkin art help her students learn to read, write, and speak? She had to admit to herself that nothing about the pumpkin activity achieved those goals.

Melinda knew something needed to change if her students were to achieve the outcome she was after. It hurt her heart to get rid of her beloved activity because it didn't have the impact she wanted. How could she make this great activity more aligned with the outcomes for her English language learners?

Instead of just creating a cute, colorful collage on a pumpkin, Melinda had her students learn and brainstorm descriptions of the pumpkin instead. Then they took these descriptions and created a paragraph story with them. A rubric assessed the reading level the students used for their stories. The students still had fun and still got to be creative, but the academic rigor increased significantly.

What Melinda learned from this experience is that the best lessons take preparation, planning, and an effort to align with the results desired. Instead of starting with the activity and *hoping* it would build skills, she started with the standards or objectives she had to achieve. Then she looked at how those objectives were going to be assessed to ensure that the skill and activity she planned for students would check off the skills her students were supposed to demonstrate on their assessment.

Coaching sessions work the same way. What is the desired outcome for the coaching session? How will the coachee's assessment determine if that outcome is met? Now, how will the session be set up? What kinds of topics need to be covered, questions asked, and tasks assigned and completed that would most effectively get the coachee to their outcomes?

COACHING SCHOOL LEADERS IS A POWERFUL ACT OF LEADERSHIP ITSELF.

Complex by nature, but guided by a strong framework, it becomes the catalyst for transformational change.

In an attempt to synthesize everything we know about coaching for education leaders, we've set up a framework of action items below as a starting point for planning. Don't worry; we're not having you construct pumpkins here. In fact, it's quite simple.

Coaching school leaders is anything but simple, but that's exactly why we created the SIMPLE Coaching Framework: to bring clarity, focus, and intention to a complex process.

SIMPLE stands for Support, Inspire, Measure, Personalize, Listen, and Empower. The SIMPLE Coaching Framework establishes a successful platform for both the coach and the coachee to ensure success on both ends and offers a structured path to guide the work with purpose and precision. Think of them as the key performance indicators (KPIs) of coaching, the key indicators that the coach is doing what coaches do. If the coachee has their set of accountability structures, this is the coach's accountability. To coach successfully, it's essential to anchor each session in the SIMPLE Coaching Framework, both when planning ahead and reflecting afterward. Coaches should identify which indicators were present in the session, recognize which were missing, and determine ways to better align future sessions with the framework to strengthen their impact. Think of it as a rubric for coaching. If you are fulfilling each part of the SIMPLE Coaching Framework, you're most likely doing well as a coach.

COACHING FRAMEWORK

Support
- Provide guidance and encouragement
- Create space for self-discovery
- Identify behaviors, values, beliefs, and biases to deeply explore "Why"
- Apply ongoing intentional encouragement

Inspire
- Spark motivation and confidence
- Identify and celebrate quick wins
- Establish and monitor goals
- Engage in reflection

Measure
- Establish a coaching cadence and confidence
- Guide and track goal progress
- Track long-term achievements
- Communicate progress to stakeholders within the organization

Personalize
- Customize approach to individual needs
- Connect daily behaviors to deeper purpose
- Leverage strengths and areas for growth
- Assess, adjust, and refine coaching

Listen
- Focus completely and listen with intent
- Understand and empathize deeply
- Invite authenticity and transparency
- Adapt to processing and reflection approach

Empower
- Cultivate self-awareness and a proactive mindset
- Build confidence and self-efficacy
- Foster ownership of growth and learning
- Solidify leadership behaviors

SIMPLE Coaching Framework

S—SUPPORT
HOW IS THE COACH SUPPORTING THE COACHEE?

Support is about providing guidance and encouragement however the coachee shows up at any given moment. As the coach, you need to hold the coachee accountable, but not in a way that feels discouraging or evaluative. Constant gentle pressure with constructive feedback is key. You can't let up and let the coachee retreat from the edge of change, but you don't want to push them over the edge where they feel like they're free-falling either. This is where trust and relationship building come into play, along with clarifying Whys, BVBs, and mindsets that are typically emphasized at the start of the coaching cycle. A coachee's Skill/Will Context also can be taken into account, as a coachee with low skill, for instance, will need more modeling and skill-building resources than someone with high skill. No matter where the coachee is on their journey, you'll be equipped to provide the right support.

I—INSPIRE
WHAT IS THE COACH DOING TO INSPIRE?

As a coach, you are an inspiration to your coachee by sparking motivation and building confidence. One powerful way to inspire is by identifying quick wins that demonstrate progress. Reflect on what the coachee has accomplished since the last session and pinpoint a success worth recognizing. This is also where a coach helps the coachee set up academic, personal, and professional goals.

Short-term goals often lead to quick wins, but longer-term goals that involve more people should be broken into smaller celebratory milestones along the way. Once a coaching relationship is established, there are moments when the coach can step into a mentoring role to add value. If the coach has experience related to an action step the coachee is working on, this is an opportunity to offer insight into what has worked well personally or what has proven effective for other leaders. By sharing relevant experiences, the coach models successful strategies and provides the coachee with practical real-world examples to consider.

Inspiration in coaching sparks purpose, energy, and possibility, helping the coachee overcome limitations and take meaningful action. It builds trust, fosters growth, and deepens the coaching relationship, empowering the coachee to embrace challenges with confidence.

M—MEASURE
HOW WILL THE COACHEE'S ACTIONS BE MEASURED?

Our focus on results-driven coaching emphasizes measuring progress and the outcomes achieved. If the coachee is making progress, great, we need to do more of what we're doing. If progress is not being made, adjustments may be necessary to achieve the desired results. This could include changing the frequency of sessions, such as moving from biweekly to weekly meetings. Or maybe the coachee needs more time in between to accomplish tasks, so a once-a-month session would be better. We want to do what is achievable for the coachee and what works with their capacity and collaboration style.

The Measure part of the framework is mostly about monitoring and measuring progress according to objective criteria. The goals are being achieved, and the data over time at the school, state, and federal levels provides valuable insight. Third-party assessments, as well as pre- and post-reflections, offer further evidence of progress and outcomes. Whatever goal the coachee picks to achieve, the milestones to that achievement must be measured objectively.

The communication part is important, partly because we want to be able to celebrate regular milestones achieved. Those quick wins provide morale boosts and good incentive to keep momentum going. They also give quick indicators to see if the plan or coaching needs adjustment along the way before a final assessment is due and a crisis occurs because things still aren't done and now there's no time to do them.

P—PERSONALIZE
WHAT IS THE COACH DOING TO PERSONALIZE THE COACHING EXPERIENCE?

The Personalize criterion is about ensuring the coaching remains tailored to the individual coachee's needs and preferences. The coachee's BVBs, mindset, skill and will, strengths, and collaboration styles all need to be taken into account to determine the coaching style and feedback method the coachee will most appreciate and work well with.

This personalized approach to coaching and the attention brought to strengths will also develop the coachee's leadership style and skills. In which areas of leadership is the coachee most comfortable or do they want to grow? These can then be incorporated into their goals, actions plans, and future behaviors, all with a wider goal of increasing their growth mindset and flexibility. Periodically, the coach will want to revisit the coachee's Why as well as their strengths and collaboration preferences, established during the first session, to see how they've changed and to see if the coach needs to shift coaching styles to better match the coachee's way of thinking and working.

L—LISTEN
WHAT IS THE COACH DOING TO LISTEN ACTIVELY TO THE COACHEE?

Listening actively is all about understanding and empathizing with your coachee. The active listener explores the words their coachee says, explores the emotions behind those words. They can pick up on the energy shifts between the coach and coachee and both verbal and nonverbal communication and behaviors. Most importantly, they don't interrupt. If you listen well, empathy and understanding will follow.

Stephen Covey says "most people do not listen with the intent to understand; they listen with the intent to reply." Someone listening to understand seeks to be able to accurately paraphrase and get at the intentions and meanings of the person doing the talking. It is an exercise in curiosity and compassion. Someone listening to respond, however, seeks to filter out anything that does not already agree with the listener's point of view so the listener can come back with their own opinion and "win" the conversation. Or the "listening" is merely a waiting game, and the listener is paying lip service to the speaker until it is the listener's turn to talk. When someone listens to respond, they aren't really interested in what the other person has to say or where they are coming from. Again, this goes back to respecting a coachee's stories, BVBs, and Why. A coach must be flexible and tolerant of many points of view even if the coach thinks they are wrong. Gentle pressure with constructive feedback, probing, curiosity, and hard evidence will hopefully iron out any ideas that won't work and dispel any preconceived notions the coach or coachee may take into a session.

Sometimes a coachee just needs empathy. When a coachee says to you "I have a challenge," sometimes all they want is for you, a neutral, experienced third party, to acknowledge their pain: "Yes, that does sound challenging." As leaders and coaches, we want to jump to the solution right away. We want to give advice. But you don't want to do that with somebody who doesn't want a coach at the moment, who wants a friend.

> IT CAN BE LONELY IN A LEADERSHIP ROLE, AND SOMETIMES THE BEST THING YOU CAN DO IS TO LISTEN AND ACKNOWLEDGE HOW HARD AND SLOW CHANGE CAN BE.

E—EMPOWER
HOW IS THE COACH EMPOWERING THE COACHEE TO TAKE CHARGE OF THEIR OWN LEADERSHIP DEVELOPMENT?

The whole point of coaching is to help leaders grow by turning reflection into action, challenges into opportunities, and potential into impact. The ultimate goal of any coach is to get their coachee to a place where they have the soft skills and confidence to own their own personal development and the development of their faculty, staff, school, and/or district. The coachee evolves from learner to leader—able to spot challenges and drive change independently. They can leverage their strengths and transfer their leadership skills from one role to the next. And they can become coaches themselves and take over coaching up the next generation of leaders, thereby creating a sustainable leadership pipeline in their school and district. They can create long-lasting system-level change as autonomous leaders.

As a coach, your role is to empower the coachee to take the lead in their own development—shifting from guided support to independent problem-solving. Encourage them to reflect critically, make decisions, and assess what's working and what's not. Instead of providing all the answers, create space for them to explore solutions and take meaningful ownership of their growth. This builds their confidence, sharpens their leadership instincts, and helps them become self-sufficient in driving progress.

Keep in mind that the SIMPLE Coaching Framework is not a linear process; it's a continuous, flexible flow of planning, doing, and reflecting. There's no clear start or finish line. Instead, it's built on key levers that can be activated at any time, depending on the needs of the leader and the moment. Coaching isn't about checking boxes in order; it's about knowing which move to make next to keep growth moving forward.

CONCLUSION

The SIMPLE Coaching Framework works like formative assessments—it's ongoing, responsive, and built to adjust in real time.

> **YOU DON'T WAIT FOR A FINAL GRADE TO COURSE-CORRECT; YOU SUPPORT GROWTH EVERY STEP OF THE WAY.**

If you go slow in the beginning of the coaching relationship, you make up for it in the end in fewer hiccups along the way. It isn't like you have to go into the first session and light the world on fire. You build the relationship, acknowledge and validate the coachee's story, and set some goals and offer some strategies. By the third or fourth session, you're rocking and rolling.

SIMPLE is the cornerstone of change management in education spaces. All indicators in the SIMPLE Coaching Framework can be implemented at any time in the coaching flow or session. You may find yourself going back to one, such as Support, a few times during a session. The end goal is always that you, as coach, will be pulling these various levers for change less and less as the coachee takes on more and more leadership skills and knowledge and they internalize their own coaching mindset, which gets to the final goal: the leader becomes a coach for others behind them.

TOOL: THE SIMPLE COACHING FRAMEWORK REFLECTION

Purpose: To assess how intentionally you are applying each element of the SIMPLE Coaching Framework in your coaching practice and identify next steps to grow.

Support

How do I provide consistent support without overdirecting?

How do I adjust support based on skill/will?

My Strengths: _____

My Growth Areas: _____

Next Step: _____

Inspire

How do I highlight quick wins or growth moments?

How do I spark motivation or confidence during coaching sessions?

My Strengths: _____

My Growth Areas: _____

Next Step: _____

Measure

How am I tracking progress toward goals?

Do I adjust strategies when progress stalls?

My Strengths: _____

My Growth Areas: _____

Next Step: _____

Personalize

How do I tailor coaching to the coachee's values, strengths, and collaboration style?

When was the last time I revisited their Why?

My Strengths: _____

My Growth Areas: _____

Next Step: _____

Listen

Do I listen to understand or to respond?

How do I show empathy when the coachee is struggling?

My Strengths: _____

My Growth Areas: _____

Next Step: _____

Empower

How do I help the coachee take ownership of their growth?

What steps am I taking to build their autonomy as a leader?

My Strengths: _____

My Growth Areas: _____

Next Step: _____

Final Prompt

Which element of the SIMPLE Coaching Framework do you want to grow in the most this month? What specific action will you take to strengthen it in your next one to two coaching sessions?

PART 4

Creating a Coaching System

CHAPTER 9

The Flow of Coaching

"Coaching is not a one-size-fits-all process. It's about finding the right rhythm—sometimes fast, sometimes slow, but always purposeful and in tune with the coachee's needs."
—Marshall Goldsmith, author

Principal Martinez was burning out. Her days were packed with hallway supervision, behavior referrals, and a dozen unfinished coaching plans. When Lorna arrived for their monthly session, Principal Martinez sighed. "Let me guess; we're supposed to review that feedback tracker I never filled out?"

Lorna smiled gently. "Actually, I thought we'd talk about how we're structuring our time together and how it's working for you."

Principal Martinez paused. "Wow, no one's asked me that before. Let me think about this."

They took ten minutes to map out the coaching flow: short weekly check-ins, a two-week cadence for observing and practicing feedback conversations, and a shared goal that felt manageable.

By the next session, Principal Martinez had completed her tracker, not out of compliance, but because the rhythm made sense. Coaching was no longer "another thing"; it was the thing helping her stay grounded.

> **COACHING ISN'T JUST SUPPORT; IT'S STRATEGY. WHEN DONE CONSISTENTLY, IT BECOMES THE BACKBONE OF REAL, LASTING CHANGE.**

The coaching flow provides a clear, intentional structure that guides the entire journey, from building momentum and deepening impact to driving lasting change. At the start of each session, the coach will review where the coachee is in the process, often beginning with a check-in on how things have been progressing and what has come up during their recent work. These reflections deepen the coach-coachee relationship and help the coach identify areas that need attention or follow-up. For example, after reviewing the previous session's tasks, the coach might ask, "How did your walkthroughs go? What did you learn from them?" The goal is to assess progress and ensure that tasks are being completed as expected.

BUILDING TRUST

A coaching journey is a structured series of sessions designed to help a school or district leader achieve a specific, measurable outcome. Each coaching journey unfolds over multiple sessions, tailored to the complexity of the goal, the pace of progress, time availability, and budget considerations.

In *The Speed of Trust*, Stephen Covey argues that trust is a critical, measurable asset that drives efficiency, reduces costs, and enhances relationships.[26] Covey outlines five waves of trust that build outward from the individual to the broader world, emphasizing that trust must first be cultivated within before it can extend effectively to others.

The first wave, *self-trust*, centers on personal credibility, honesty, competence, and alignment with one's values.

The second wave, *relationship trust*, focuses on consistent behavior that builds strong connections through integrity, transparency, and respect.

The third wave, *organizational trust*, involves creating systems, structures, and cultures within institutions that foster trust among teams and stakeholders.

The fourth wave, *market trust*, is about establishing a strong reputation and brand based on consistent performance and ethical behavior in the marketplace.

Finally, the fifth wave, *societal trust*, refers to contributing to the greater good by acting in ways that benefit the community and build confidence in institutions and leadership on a broader scale. Each wave builds on the previous one, reinforcing the idea that trust starts from within and radiates outward to influence larger systems. Covey emphasizes that trust can be built and maintained through thirteen key behaviors, such as transparency, respect, and accountability. Ultimately, trust is both an economic driver and a foundational principle for personal and organizational success.

The initial session can make or break the relationship in terms of trust. Covey says trust is reciprocal, and when

---

[26] Stephen M. R. Covey, and Rebecca R. Merrill *The Speed of Trust: The One Thing That Changes Everything* (Free Press, 2006).

broken, it can be restored through consistent, intentional actions. We've read elsewhere that a person has ten seconds to make a good first impression. If it's not a good impression, you need fifteen or twenty more encounters to shift that negative first impression and regain trust.

It takes many instances to build trust, but it takes only one instance to lose it. And for a coach, the only way to have an effective coaching flow is with trust. The first coaching session is all about building the relationship through trust, and there are a few topics and types of questions that are always useful to get to this goal.

SETTING EXPECTATIONS

The first session is dedicated to building that foundational trust and establishing expectations for both the coach and the coachee. Clear communication of roles and responsibilities is essential—both parties need to understand their obligations and what is expected in terms of progress and tasks. This session lays out not only the coachee's responsibilities, but also the coach's role in providing support, guidance, and accountability. Setting the stage for these expectations ensures that the coachee knows exactly when their tasks are considered complete and how they can track progress.

Additionally, this session involves determining accountability structures that work best for the coachee. Together, the coach and coachee will decide on assessment tools, timelines, and check-ins that are aligned with the coachee's goals. While reward and accountability systems can be helpful, the emphasis in the coaching relationship is on how the coachee will reflect on and evaluate the effectiveness of their actions in a thoughtful and supportive way. This collaborative process typically takes place during the second session, when the coachee's action plan is also created.

CREATING SOFT ACCOUNTABILITY

In a strong coaching relationship, accountability doesn't need to feel harsh or punitive; it should feel supportive, clear, and purposeful. One of the most important elements of this is ensuring that the coachee understands exactly what is expected of them. This includes having clearly defined tasks, timelines, and success criteria written out in black and white. When expectations are transparent, it builds trust and allows the coachee to confidently move forward, knowing what they are responsible for and how their progress will be measured.

Both the coach and the coachee play active roles in this process. The coach supports, guides, and checks in, while the coachee takes ownership of the work. This dual clarity helps eliminate confusion and fosters a sense of shared responsibility. Soft accountability means that while the coachee is held to their commitments, they are also encouraged and supported through challenges, with the coach providing reflection, redirection, or realignment as needed.

This process typically begins during the creation of the action plan, often in the second coaching session, where tasks, benchmarks, and timelines are codeveloped. From that point on, each session circles back to this plan to assess progress, celebrate wins, troubleshoot roadblocks, and adjust next steps. This structure empowers the coachee to stay focused and motivated while reinforcing the coaching flow that supports long-term growth.

KEEPING THE FLOW ALIVE

After the initial session, where you build the relationship and set the focus for the coaching flow, you must keep the flow alive. A flow structure helps maintain consistency and ensures that both coach and coachee stay aligned and intentional in their work together. Regularly refer back to the SIMPLE Coaching Framework as your guide; it will help you stay focused on the agreed-upon goals and ensure each session builds toward meaningful progress. Continue this flow until the end of the coach's allotted time with the coachee, keeping in mind that formal coaching, especially when funded by a school or district, typically operates within a defined time frame.

The results of any coaching flow are dual: to improve systems and improve the coachee's leadership skills, so while these steps are the general pattern of our coaching flow, yours may not follow it exactly, and that's okay.

Finally, there are three C's to keep in mind throughout the coaching flow: clarity, consistency, and continued feedback. Clarity defines clear goals and expectations to guide the coaching process and ensure everyone understands the direction. Consistency maintains a regular, reliable coaching schedule and approach to build trust and reinforce growth. Continued feedback provides constructive, actionable critique that promotes ongoing learning, reflection, and improvement.

COACHING IN REAL TIME

A principal calls Melinda midweek, overwhelmed by a staff conflict that's escalating and impacting morale.

"Thanks for reaching out," Melinda says. "Let's take a breath and look at what's happening. What have you tried so far? What's your goal for resolving this, both short term and long term?"

As the principal talks it out, Melinda listens actively, then offers, "Sounds like this might be a good time to revisit how you've set expectations for communication with your team. How might we use this moment to reinforce your leadership message and rebuild trust?"

Together, they map out a quick action plan: a staff listening session, a follow-up communication to clarify norms, and a strategy for checking in with key team members afterward.

Coaching often involves working through immediate real-time problems. These "problems of practice" can range from staffing shortages and team dynamics to instructional gaps and leadership decisions that demand urgent attention. Unlike long-term planning or theoretical conversations, these issues require the coach and coachee to pivot in the moment, focusing on what's pressing now. This doesn't mean abandoning the broader coaching flow; it means leaning into the reality of leadership, where flexibility and responsiveness are essential.

In these situations, the coach becomes a thought partner, helping the coachee pause, reflect, and unpack what's happening beneath the surface. Together, they identify root causes, explore options, and strategize next steps, often while balancing the emotional weight that comes with high-stakes decisions. These conversations are often messy, unpredictable, and deeply human, but they are also where some of the most powerful coaching happens.

Rather than disrupting the coaching process, these real-time challenges actually enrich it. They build trust, demonstrate the coach's commitment to supporting the coachee where they are, and underscore the iterative nature of leadership growth. Over time, these responsive moments begin to shape how coachees approach all aspects of their work: with more confidence, clarity, and the ability to self-coach through complexity.

WHEN THINGS GET STUCK

Principal Lopez has been working on strengthening staff culture. The focus of these coaching sessions is to build more authentic collaboration during collaborative meetings. Today, the session feels flat. The principal is answering questions, but with little energy or depth. Lorna notices a lack of momentum and engagement.

"I'm noticing we're talking through strategies, but something feels a bit off from where we left off last session," Lorna begins. "Can I check in? How are you feeling about the progress since our last conversation?"

Principal Lopez shrugs slightly. "I mean…I did a few of the things we talked about. Teacher meetings are happening. I shared a protocol. But I don't know. It's not really landing."

Lorna gets curious. "That's helpful to hear. When you say 'not landing,' what makes you feel that way?"

Principal Lopez explains, "People are participating, but there's no real dialogue. It still feels like they're just doing it to check the box."

Lorna allows a pause for reflection, then says, "Hmm. I wonder if we can zoom out for a moment. When we started focusing on meetings, what was the bigger impact you were hoping for?"

Principal Lopez wrinkles his brow in thought. "I wanted teams to feel like they owned the work together," he says slowly, "and it's not just me driving it. More collaboration, less compliance."

"That's a strong vision," Lorna affirms. "Could it be something in the structure? The modeling? Maybe the purpose needs to be reclarified with the team?" she probes.

Nodding slowly, Principal Lopez gets even more thoughtful. "Maybe it's the purpose piece. I assumed people knew why we were doing it, but I don't think I've really revisited that with them."

Encouraging now, Lorna asks, "What if the next step isn't about the protocol, but about reconnecting the team to the Why? Would you be open to designing a short opener for your next meeting to reground everyone in the purpose?"

With more energy, Principal Lopez nods. "Yeah, I could do that. It might help shift the vibe."

Although the principal didn't say, "I'm stuck," Lorna noticed the lack of progress and energy and shifted the tone of the session using curiosity, perspective taking, and the SIMPLE Coaching Framework as a guide for reflection. This helped the principal uncover where alignment was missing and choose a more impactful next step over which he felt ownership.

Inevitably, there will be moments when the coaching process stalls or loses momentum. These pauses are not failures; they are part of the natural rhythm of any meaningful growth journey.

WHEN A SESSION ISN'T GOING AS PLANNED, IT'S AN OPPORTUNITY FOR THE COACH TO PAUSE, REFLECT, AND RECALIBRATE WITH INTENTIONALITY.

These moments call for curiosity rather than judgment, allowing both the coach and the coachee to explore what might be causing the disconnect.

The reasons for a stall can vary: goals may have been too ambitious or too vague, competing priorities might have emerged, or the coachee may be feeling overwhelmed, discouraged, or disengaged. Instead of pushing forward without clarity, effective coaches slow down to listen deeply, ask reflective questions, and meet the coachee where they are. Sometimes this means revisiting and redefining goals; breaking larger objectives into smaller, more achievable steps; or shifting strategies to reignite energy and progress.

At times like this, it's important to reflect on the SIMPLE Coaching Framework to identify which area might need attention, whether that's *Support, Inspire, Measure, Personalize, Listen,* or *Empower, t*o refine the coaching flow. By revisiting the framework, the coach can pinpoint where adjustments are needed and use it as a tool to guide the process forward. In certain cases, a full "reset" session might be necessary. These sessions create space to realign expectations, reestablish trust, and reconnect to the core purpose of the coaching work. This reset can often be the turning point that brings renewed focus, deeper insight, and stronger commitment. By leaning into these moments rather than avoiding them, coaches model resilience, flexibility, and the very leadership behaviors we hope to cultivate in those we coach.

CONCLUSION

Coaching is a dynamic and evolving process that thrives on flexibility and adaptability. The most effective coaches adjust their strategies to meet the unique needs of each coachee, ensuring that the process fosters continuous growth. While clarity, consistency, and feedback serve as the foundation, exceptional coaches consistently reflect on their own practices, honing their ability to communicate, challenge, and support in ways that inspire lasting change. To continue enhancing your coaching flow and deepen your coaching skills, it's essential to regularly refer to the SIMPLE Coaching Framework and the Skill/Will chart. These tools help guide your approach, ensuring that both individual leadership development and broader systemic success are prioritized. Whether you are coaching an individual leader or a team, the ultimate aim is to build a system of ongoing improvement that drives growth, accountability, and meaningful outcomes.

TOOL: COACHING SESSION NOTES TEMPLATE

Coachee: _____ School/District: _____

Role/Title: _____ Date: _____

Coach: _____

Session Focus/Agenda *What is the main topic or goal for this session? (Established by leader or coach)*

- _____
- _____

Leadership Development Focus Area(s) *Check all that apply:*

- Vision and Strategic Planning
- Instructional Leadership
- Equity and Culture
- Talent Development and Staffing
- Systems and Operations
- Communication and Influence
- Personal Leadership/Growth
- Crisis/Change Management
- Other: _____

Key Discussion Highlights *What insights, challenges, or reflections came up during the session?*

- _____
- _____
- _____

Breakthroughs and Wins *Any success, clarity, or progress the leader made since the last session?*

- _____
- _____

Barriers/Obstacles Identified *What's getting in the way of progress?*

- _____
- _____

Action Steps/Commitments *What are the leader's next steps before the next session?*

ACTION STEP	RESPONSIBLE PARTY	DUE DATE	NOTES

Skill/Will Matrix Reflection (Optional) *Where is the leader on the task discussed today?*

TASK/GOAL	LOW SKILL/ LOW WILL	LOW SKILL/ HIGH WILL	HIGH SKILL/ VARIABLE WILL	HIGH SKILL/ HIGH WILL

Coach's Reflections and Next Steps *What themes or patterns are emerging? What should the coach prepare for next time?*

- _____
- _____

COACHING FRAMEWORK

Support
- Provide guidance and encouragement
- Create space for self-discovery
- Identify behaviors, values, beliefs, and biases to deeply explore "Why"
- Apply ongoing intentional encouragement

S

Inspire
- Spark motivation and confidence
- Identify and celebrate quick wins
- Establish and monitor goals
- Engage in reflection

I

Measure
- Establish a coaching cadence and confidence
- Guide and track goal progress
- Track long-term achievements
- Communicate progress to stakeholders within the organization

M

Personalize
- Customize approach to individual needs
- Connect daily behaviors to deeper purpose
- Leverage strengths and areas for growth
- Assess, adjust, and refine coaching

P

Listen
- Focus completely and listen with intent
- Understand and empathize deeply
- Invite authenticity and transparency
- Adapt to processing and reflection approach

L

Empower
- Cultivate self-awareness and a proactive mindset
- Build confidence and self-efficacy
- Foster ownership of growth and learning
- Solidify leadership behaviors

E

CHAPTER 10

A Culture of Coaching

"Coaching is one of the most effective leadership styles that can transform, empower and unlock people's potential. Ask more, give advice less, and elevate your impact forever."

—FARSHAD ASL, AUTHOR

When we first sat down with Superintendent Smith of a large urban district, he wasted no time laying out his vision for "transformation."

"We need to cut two hundred people," he said, his voice cold and resolute. "That's the only way forward. Clean house. Reset the culture. No half measures."

It was clear that he equated change with clearing the slate. But we paused and asked, "And who's lining up to take those two hundred jobs? Are they better qualified and ready to lead on day one?"

There was a long silence.

That moment became the pivot. Instead of wiping the slate clean, we offered a different path: What if, instead of replacing people, we invested in them? What if coaching became the transformation and a new culture of support and growth replaced the old dysfunctional culture?

> **A COACHING CULTURE SHIFTS THE FOCUS FROM FIXING PEOPLE TO EMPOWERING THEM—AND THAT CHANGES EVERYTHING.**

In coaching leaders, two timeless insights hold profound lessons on the forces that shape organizational success. Peter Drucker's famous observation, "Culture eats strategy for breakfast," and W. Edwards Deming's equally insightful statement, "Every system is perfectly designed to get the results it gets," serve as powerful reminders that leaders must look beyond strategy alone to truly drive lasting impact.

Consider the superintendent who believed replacing people was the answer. That mindset had already seeped into the district's organizational culture, creating a tense, fear-driven environment. Staff were constantly looking over their shoulders, unsure if they'd be next. When fear becomes the dominant emotion in a workplace, collaboration fades, risk-taking disappears, and innovation stalls. What does it say about the culture? It says that survival, not growth, has become the priority. Who wants to try harder for an organization that doesn't appreciate them? And no true transformation can happen in a culture where people are more focused on protecting themselves than improving outcomes for students.

Here, Drucker's quote comes into play. What the leader failed to realize is that culture, not strategy, dictates the true behavior of the organization. The company culture, rooted in risk aversion and a fear of failure, has created an unspoken barrier to innovation. Despite the brilliant strategy on paper, the culture beneath it has not shifted to support the boldness required for innovation to thrive. In this case, the culture is the silent yet dominant force that derails the strategy before it can even get off the ground.

In coaching the leader above, the first step is making them aware of the deep influence culture has on outcomes. Without aligning the culture to embrace experimentation, collaboration, and even the potential for failure, any strategy focused on innovation will struggle. The coach's role here is to guide the leader in recognizing the gap between their strategy and the organizational culture and to help them foster an environment that supports the behaviors they want to see.

To make coaching sustainable across not just a school but a school district, larger systems that set up a coaching habit need to be put in place across the organization. The focus should be on coaching that builds the institutional will to support the development of skills that will be retained and applied long term. In short, creating a system for culture means focusing on how leadership shapes and improves organizational dynamics, such as feedback, rather than addressing isolated issues.

IDENTIFYING SYSTEMS THROUGH COACHING

During a tour of all the classrooms in one school, Lorna and Melinda's coaching group observed a teacher doing collaborative learning where all the students were spaced out around the room working in groups to solve a problem. In the next classroom there was none of this. The principal then shared that the teachers had just had some professional development training on how to implement student engagement with group work.

"How many rooms did we see this new technique being used in?" Melinda asked. Everyone counted it up. Only two out of twenty. "Why do you think that is?"

"Well, they went to the professional development training; they should do it," the principal said, as if it were that simple.

"But what system do you have in place to support the implementation of that technique? What expectation about implementation did you share? Are they supposed to do this once a month, once a week, or only when they feel like it? Is there a system of accountability?"

"Good questions," the principal admitted.

It was the training scenario Melinda liked to use in workshops all over again, where the principals are inclined to first blame the teachers for lack of implementation and sustainability with learned professional development strategies. But is it really the teachers' fault if only the What is communicated but not the When, Where, How, and Why?

The goals for coaching are first to help coachees identify their values and strengths to help them grow. That's finding strengths as an individual on the personal level. Then the coach can help the coachees find the strengths for the other people on their teams. Then there's that higher level, where the coachee must identify strengths at the system level. How is the coachee going to build on all those personal strengths to build up the system?

At its best, coaching for leaders is geared toward the systems they are in charge of implementing and running. What's the system that the coachee has in place for curriculum instruction? What are the processes and actions in place for growing teachers or ensuring teachers follow the curriculum? Or growing principals and ensuring they adhere to the district's strategic plan? Where's the system failure that creates ineffective behavior or outcomes? Is there a failure in an existing system, or is there no system at all to support the outcome? Maybe there's a support system, like an annual training, to be put in place to correct this failure.

Coaching sessions not only support the coachee and leader, but the systems that that coachee is responsible for creating, implementing, and, yes, institutionalizing. Just as good teachers don't blame individual students for failure but a failure in the system that raised and taught them, good leaders don't blame individual faculty and staff for things not getting done. The buck stops at the top. If something isn't happening that should be happening, then there's a lack of instructional infrastructure to operationalize and support that ongoing action. That means the system—the culture—has to change before individual people can change. And one of the simplest ways to change a culture is to change the way leaders give feedback.

DEFINING FEEDBACK

Feedback in the coaching world is the preferred means of growth and the move toward independent problem-solving. A book by two Harvard professors, Douglas Stone and Sheila Heen, called *Thanks for the Feedback*, describes types of feedback that can fall into three groups: evaluation, praise, and constructive feedback. The professors describe evaluative feedback as summative. As a final score or assessment of performance, there's really nothing further to do with it. In the case of coaching, evaluative feedback looks like the checklist of things the coachee needs to work on as a leader. Its biggest job is to make the coachee aware of what they need to improve, but it doesn't help the coachee make these improvements.

The next type of feedback is praise, the "good job" type of feedback. But if the exact details of what the coachee did is left out, they don't get an idea of what they did that was good and why. Say Lorna goes into a classroom and says to the teacher she's coaching, "You have a conducive learning environment" and walks out again. Well, what the heck was that? What made it "conducive"? Conducive to what? Why is that important? Is the teacher even aware of the classroom techniques she used that created that environment?

The third type of feedback, of course, is constructive feedback. Melinda meets with a school leader and says, "Consider focusing not only on staff retention but also on addressing underlying systemic issues to create a sustainable and positive culture within the school community." What does that strategy look like? How do you make that happen? And even though all of us as educators *say* we like constructive feedback, it's still hard to swallow, as it points out areas we could improve and, depending on how it is delivered, may sound condescending or unhelpful if not enough context is given or it is given in a summative context, say at the end of a project when there is no opportunity to revise or redo.

It's always nerve-racking at the beginning, when you get feedback from a new person. Once a relationship is in place, feedback becomes easier to give and take. It's easier for both sides to acknowledge what didn't go well and think through a solution for how tasks can be tweaked next time for better results. In order for you, as a coach, to give a coachee constructive feedback that lands and is used, there has to be trust in the relationship. Only through trust can you finally give that constructive feedback and have it be implemented.

Feedback has to be helpful, a way to move toward something, not just point out what's wrong in the moment. As a funnier example, if an Airbnb review says you have to mow the lawn, that's telling and doesn't give a reason why mowing the lawn is desired. If, however, the review says more people would go to the lake if there was a better-mown path to it, that's more along the lines of constructive feedback. Construct, of course, means you are building something, making something better. The second review explains how the rental could be better so the renter could get more guests.

Or, for an example closer to home, the coach and coachee complete a classroom walkthrough. Now, the coach could say, "Here's what I saw needs to be improved," which falls into that telling/evaluative area. Or the coach could invite collaborative problem-solving afterward: "Hey, let's debrief. What do you think we saw going on there? What's an area we can focus on to improve?" Constructive feedback, then, works best in instructional and collaborative coaching, where the goal is to build a leader up so they can step up and take the lead.

The best kind of feedback comes straight from the coachee: "I'm seeing my staff do this when they should be doing that. I think there needs to be a change there." That kind of feedback produces more follow-through as it was the coachee's idea and probably related to their strengths and values.

A coach's biggest tools are open-ended, empowering questions that allow coachees to reflect. How you ask those questions as a coach makes the difference between success and failure, between sounding directive and biased to sounding collaborative and open to everyone's BVBs.

FEEDBACK TO GROW

The prospect of getting feedback, like going to the principal's office, creates no end of anxiety for people, many of whom expect the kind of criticism that only notes what's going wrong and doesn't focus on what's going right or focus on areas that the person being evaluated wants to improve. The mindset shifts from evaluative to constructive. How does feedback build a coachee up and show them how to improve next time? How do you give feedback in a way that is both received and acted upon? How can feedback help shift from a culture of compliance and hesitation to one of trust, support, and continuous growth?

Telling someone what to do may get someone to do something once, but they won't understand why or how they are being told to do this thing and usually resist doing it again. Now, if the telling is paired with demonstrations of how to do something and a quick explanation of why it's important, then a good habit may be formed. For instance, we teach children how to wash their hands by (1) saying it gets rid of germs that can make them sick, (2) showing them how to wash their hands, and (3) coaching them through the handwashing process a few times.

But if the task isn't simple and straightforward, telling and demonstrating gets rather tedious and prescriptive. How *would* you "tell" someone—and demonstrate!—how to set up a "conducive learning environment" in a few words? That's a little more complicated than "rub your hands together and scrub under all your nails with warm water and soap as you count to thirty." That being said, there are times when telling saves a lot of time, particularly when a leader is about to go down a path you know research has shown is ineffective. You don't want them to waste time on that particular mistake, so you tell them, "Research has shown…" But you don't get stuck on the teaching here; you use it as a springboard to move on to more lucrative conversations. Coaches shouldn't tell more than 20 percent of the time so the coaching doesn't turn into pure directive coaching.

Advice relates to what someone should or should not do in a particular situation. It can be well received for particular tasks or goals if the advice is solicited by the coachee with the old "What should I do?" But going down this trail too long can lead to the coachee becoming dependent on the coach's all-knowing words, rendering the coachee more follower than leader. If you always tell somebody what to do, what do they do when you're gone? What do they do if they go somewhere else or to a new role? As a coach, you want to help people grow. You want it to be sustainable. If you coach for a year, you want your coachee to continue to make progress once you're gone. In the end, the coachee must be able to transfer some of the skills learned through coaching from one context to the next.

Advice can also be unsolicited and ill-timed. The coachee may not want or welcome someone else making suggestions on what they should do; they feel they are being preached to or a finger is being wagged in their face. So in a coaching situation, while giving advice to "help" someone may be very tempting (especially when we already know what works!), we have to allow space for the coachee to help themselves by saying "I'm not sure. What do you think you should do?"

If the coachee is truly stuck and starting to spin their wheels because they don't know enough to problem-solve themselves, a coach can offer advice modestly with a well-placed "I" statement: "Well, what I did here was this. What they did there was that." The coachee can then select a solution from this small buffet of choices and take ownership over it.

The thing to remember is to always defer to the coachee on the solution they want to try. "Your situation may be different from mine. You're in a small stand-alone K–12 school. I was in a huge school district in a major city. What do you think will work for you?" The decision is still in their control.

THE VOICE OF A LEADERSHIP COACH ISN'T THE LOUDEST IN THE ROOM; IT'S THE ONE THAT HELPS OTHERS FIND THEIRS.

Coaches plant seeds. They encourage reflection. The coachee has to have practices and systems in place that can continue to sustain growth once we're gone. Whereas if we just tell you what to do and leave, guess what you're going to do when we leave? Nothing. You're going to do the same thing you did before we came. If someone wants to understand a math problem, as teachers we don't tell them the answer; we show them how to do the problem so they can solve other problems that come their way outside of our class. Same in leadership. Then it's transferable. Then it's culture. And that's a big step toward making change sustainable, but it isn't the only one.

Good coaching doesn't end when the official engagement does. That's the paradox every great coach comes to understand—there's always more to do. So when it's time to wrap up, our focus naturally shifts: What did you learn? What's your plan moving forward? How will you continue to grow independently and in collaboration with others? Coaching, when done well, creates self-sufficiency. It's not about telling someone what to do; it's about building the systems, strategies, and confidence to lead without us. That's what it means to be sustainable.

SUSTAINABILITY

Districts must ask, What needs to change at the system level to support not just one school, but all twenty-five under your supervision? You can't be in every building, but you can develop leaders who know how to run each one effectively. Coaching aligns people to the district's strategic plan, connects goals to real systems of support, and generates the kind of feedback that leads to real, lasting improvement no matter who fills the top roles.

Sustainability in leadership begins with coaching up school and district leaders to become more effective leader-coaches who not only lead well but also grow the next generation of leaders. There's a common misconception that once someone reaches the central office, their credentials alone qualify them for success. But every promotion comes with a new learning curve, and often a sense of imposter syndrome. Just because a leader can manage budgets or oversee staffing doesn't mean they're equipped to communicate effectively, manage large-scale change, or lead with clarity at the next level. Some leaders excel in one context but struggle when the complexity increases.

This is where coaching makes a difference. Coaching doesn't teach someone how to do their job—that's what training and credentials are for—but it does help them perform their role with more confidence, clarity, and effectiveness. A coach accelerates a leader's growth, reducing missteps and preventing burnout. Coaching provides a safe space for reflection, problem-solving, and development of critical leadership traits like resilience, creativity, and strategic thinking. If coaching is considered essential for corporate executives, why wouldn't we make it available to school and district leaders?

We still coach each other to this day—because everyone needs a coach. Everyone. Maybe not every day or forever, but having someone available to help troubleshoot a problem, refine a strategy, or process a challenge is invaluable. When coaching is institutionalized and becomes embedded in a school's or district's culture, it transforms into a renewable resource. It becomes part of the way we lead, grow, and support one another.

> **COACHING DOESN'T JUST IMPROVE PRACTICE IN THE MOMENT; IT BUILDS A SUSTAINABLE PIPELINE OF LEADERSHIP THAT ENDURES FAR BEYOND ANY ONE PERSON.**

We aim to grow leaders into coaches, at both the school and district levels, equipped with the mindsets and skills to foster meaningful change. This is how we begin to address the persistent challenges in school leadership: by investing in people, strengthening retention and promotion, boosting morale, and, most importantly, driving better outcomes for students.

Leaders want to lead, but leadership without support often leads to overwhelm. With a coach, a leader can implement meaningful change and navigate the complexity of their role without getting lost in it. And over time, coaching becomes transferable. Coached leaders become coaches themselves. They develop the mindset and the skillset to support others, keeping the flow going. That's how we build leadership pipelines, not just for individual success, but for systemic, district-wide success. Because when leaders can coach others, the work becomes transferable. It becomes embedded. It becomes culture.

CONCLUSION

We can't know what's working or why without systems that track progress over time. Coaching provides that structure. It gives us the consistency and accountability to adjust course, stay grounded in purpose, and keep growing. If districts want to strengthen every other system—instruction, equity, culture, operations—they need to start with coaching. That's how to sustain success. That's how the leadership baton keeps moving. Coaching is the system that makes all the other systems better.

TOOL: CULTURE OF COACHING REFLECTION

Purpose: Use this reflection to assess and strengthen the systems, mindsets, and habits that sustain a thriving coaching culture.

1. Current Coaching Culture

What words best describe the coaching culture in your school or district? (e.g., growth-minded, inconsistent, compliance-driven, empowering)

_____

_____

2. System Check

What school system could benefit most from consistent, high-quality coaching? (e.g., instructional practice, team collaboration, use of data)

_____

_____

3. Define Feedback

What does meaningful, growth-focused feedback look like in your context?

_____

_____

4. Sustaining the Culture

What actions are you taking—or could you take—to ensure coaching becomes embedded, not episodic?

_____

_____

Remember: *A strong coaching culture is built over time. Every conversation, every system you align, and every feedback moment helps shape it.*

Conclusion

Today's school and district leaders face immense complexity. When school leaders struggle, faculty, staff, and students feel the impact too.

LEADERS NEED RESILIENCE, STRATEGY, AND ABOVE ALL, CONNECTION.

Coaching bridges the space between aspiration and action. It nurtures clarity, builds trust, and provides the reflective space leaders need to lead with courage and purpose.

We know the best way for students to be successful is for their teachers to be successful, and we know the best way for teachers to be successful is for their leaders to be successful. A teacher may be able to eke out success in individual classrooms, but students don't stay in just one classroom with one teacher at one school. Only school leaders have the power to ensure an entire campus is set up for success for everyone.

Only district leaders have the power to ensure all campuses in their district are successful for every student matriculating through it, so that a child who does well in their elementary school can do well at their middle school and their high school and can do well wherever they go after their primary education.

We want schools and districts to thrive. We want teachers and principals to succeed. Most of all, we want students to succeed. That only happens when leaders at the helm are confident, competent, and compassionate, focused on the Whys and Hows, not just the Whats and Whens.

Effective coaching not only empowers leaders to refine their skills and strategies but also fosters a culture of continuous improvement and resilience. It equips leaders with the skills to navigate challenges, fostering adaptability and strategic alignment. It enhances emotional intelligence and decision-making capabilities, ensuring leaders can inspire and develop their teams effectively. By investing in coaching, leaders not only elevate their own capabilities but also empower their teams to achieve collective success, driving sustainable change.

At its core, coaching is about transformation, not just of systems, schools, or structures, but of people.

COACHING IS NOT A FIX FOR THE BROKEN BUT A CATALYST FOR THE WILLING.

It sharpens talent, unlocks potential, and builds the capacity for sustained leadership at every level. When embedded with intention, coaching creates a culture where growth is expected, supported, and celebrated.

The change we ask for through coaching does not ask you to adopt a totally new initiative, or reinvent the wheel, or compromise your values or identity. Instead, we've shown you how to recognize and repurpose the experiences and beliefs you already have—the ones that made you a great teacher, or counselor, or assistant principal, or principal—to a new role with a new set of challenges and priorities. To become not only the lifelong learner we know you are, but a lifelong leader. One who knows the work is never done and will keep revising and adding to your leadership skillset going forward, even as you turn around to coach the leaders coming up behind.

School and district leaders are the foundation of any educational system. Their influence shapes the success of every aspect of a school or district. When leadership is strong and communication flows effectively, the entire system benefits. By coaching to develop skilled and effective leader-coaches, we create a ripple effect that improves everything those leaders touch, ultimately leading to better student outcomes. The rewards we've seen, both for ourselves and others, affirm that the journey to developing these leaders is truly worth the effort.

If you want to continue your journey with us, visit us at www.baizaconsulting.com, click on the tab "Book," and enter the passcode "coachbetter" to check out our resources or explore our services for coaching, professional development, change management, and school transformation. Together, we'll coach better to lead better. Lead better to teach better. Teach better to make better schools.

Acknowledgments

We extend our heartfelt gratitude to the school districts, school leaders, and educators who have invited us into their communities and trusted us to support their growth. Many of you took a chance on us in the early stages of our work, and for that we are deeply grateful. Your openness, courage, and belief in partnership not only helped shape the practices shared in this book but also laid the groundwork for lasting professional relationships that continue to grow.

Special thanks to the schools and districts that opened their doors, shared their challenges, and celebrated their progress with us—your work laid the foundation for *Coach Better, Lead Better*. This book would not be possible without your partnership and dedication to continuous improvement in service of all students.

Melinda would like to acknowledge Robert Carlin, who served as her principal when she was a reading specialist in Round Rock ISD. "His encouragement to pursue leadership and continue my path by obtaining a master's degree played a pivotal role in shaping my journey."

Lorna extends her deepest gratitude to Rudy Martinez. "I wouldn't be where I am today without his guidance, mentorship, the opportunities he provided for my growth, and a lifelong friendship that continues to mean the world to me."

To my daughter, Karina, "Thank you for being the joyful light in the room and the quiet cheerleader in the background. While we sat buried in chapters and edits, you zoomed past us with a thumbs-up, silent claps, and eyes full of encouragement. You never had to say much; your presence said it all. Your love for books, just like your momma's, reminded me why we write in the first place: to inspire, to connect, and to leave something meaningful behind. You were part of every page, every pause, and every push to keep going. I'll never forget how you cheered us on, one chapter at a time. This book carries a bit of your spirit in every line."

And a special shout-out to our editor at Scribe Media, Amanda Hoppe. Thank you for keeping us focused and calm and offering just the right amount of push and pull. You cheered us on when we were sick of looking at chapter drafts and, perhaps most importantly, kept us from declaring the book "done enough" and fleeing to the beach! Your steady hand ensured this book became all we hoped it could be.

Finally, here's to us, Melinda and Lorna, to the notes we scribbled, the drafts we reworked, and the countless hours we spent coaching each other through it all. We didn't just coach better, we grew better, laughed better, and now...we toast better! Salud and cheers to the journey, the friendship, and the fact that we're still speaking to each other after writing a whole book together! Ready for book two?

About the Authors

MELINDA BAIZA is the dynamic, results-driven founder of Baiza and Associates Consulting, LLC. A certified executive coach with the International Coaching Federation (ICF), Melinda has coached school, district, and state leaders. Her approach challenges leaders to think bigger, dig deeper, and grow stronger—igniting creativity and unlocking transformative growth.

Melinda brings to her work over thirty years of experience in transforming schools and districts across the nation. Her career began in the classroom and evolved through roles such as master reading teacher, assistant principal, principal, curriculum director, assistant superintendent, and state turnaround expert. Her broad experience gives her a 360-degree view of the educational system.

Melinda is known for helping school and district leaders bring their vision to life through strategic planning, leadership development, and systems thinking. She provides targeted support in curriculum, instruction, talent management, and accountability, empowering leaders to create lasting, meaningful change. Melinda Baiza shines as a beacon of leadership, propelling educational institutions and leaders toward success one visionary step at a time.

When she's not leading transformation efforts, Melinda loves escaping to the beaches of Mexico and savoring time with her adult daughter, Karina, and her close-knit extended family—her greatest sources of joy and inspiration.

With over forty years of experience in public education, **LORNA KLOKKENGA** is a respected and dynamic leader in school transformation and leadership coaching. A former teacher, principal, and district executive, she brings a rare combination of hands-on leadership, coaching expertise, and a deep passion for student and staff success.

Lorna is a certified professional coach through the Institute for Professional Excellence in Coaching (iPEC) and is also certified by the International Coaching Federation (ICF). She specializes in leading turnaround efforts at both the campus and district levels, using her expertise to drive meaningful change and growth in educational environments. Her strategic mindset and deep commitment to equity have made her a trusted thought partner for leaders navigating complex school improvement work.

Lorna works as an educational consultant and executive coach, supporting school and district leaders across the US to strengthen leadership practices, drive improvement, and create lasting impact in their communities.

Known for her energy, clarity, and unwavering belief in what's possible, Lorna builds strong partnerships with school teams, parents, and communities. Her work continues to drive sustainable results and inspire educators to lead with both purpose and courage.

Lorna is a big believer in living fully, whether that's diving into a hard conversation, dreaming up a new strategy for school improvement, or catching a flight to somewhere warm and beautiful. Travel is her way of refueling, gaining perspective, and staying grounded in the joy that makes this work sustainable.

www.ingramcontent.com/pod-product-compliance
Lightning Source LLC
Chambersburg PA
CBHW030519080526
44586CB00011B/251